The Honeybourne Line

The continuing story of the Cheltenham to Honeybourne and Stratford upon Avon Railway

by Colin Maggs
and Peter Nicholson

1st edition

ISBN 0 907036 12 0

Published by
Line One Publishing Ltd,
Bayshill House,
Bayshill Road,
Cheltenham,
Glos.
GL50 3AA

Front cover: The Honeybourne Line's best known train — 'The Cornishman'. Seen here headed by 'Castle' class 4-6-0 No.5089 "Westminster Abbey" after leaving Hunting Butts Tunnel, with a 'Down' working on 1st August 1962. (W. Potter)

Rear cover: Toddington, 30th September 1984. Former BR class 14 0-6-0 diesel hydraulic No.D9537, as beautifully restored in BR green livery by its owners, the Cotswold Diesel Preservation Group. It was acquired from British Steel Corporation, Corby, Northants and arrived on the GWR 23rd November 1982. (P.D. Nicholson)

The informative station nameboard at Honeybourne Junction. Although the line from Cheltenham to Stratford upon Avon has always been known as the "Honeybourne Line", this station was not in fact on the line, but on the Worcester to Oxford route and trains reached it by means of a connecting curve. (L.B. Lapper)

Contents

CHELTENHAM & STRATFORD LINE.

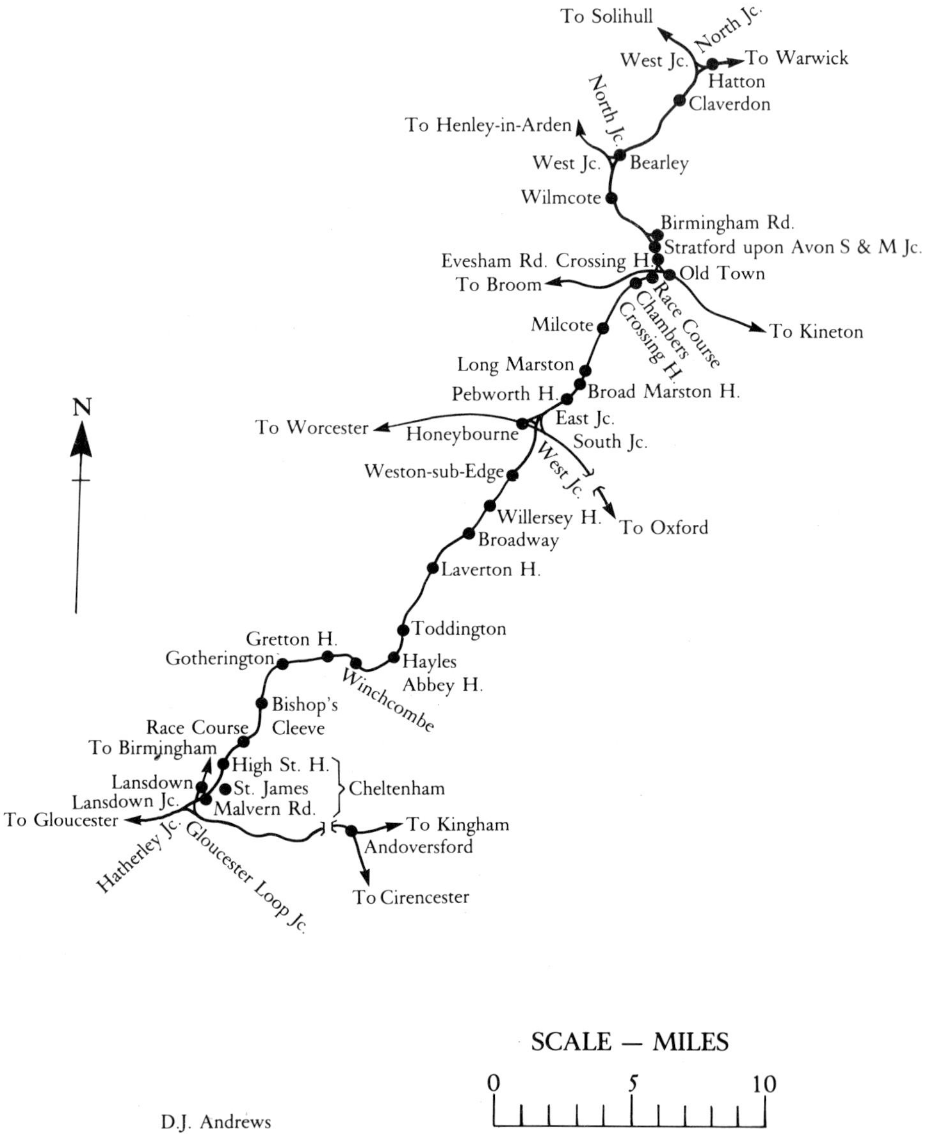

To Solihull
North Jc.
West Jc.
To Warwick
Hatton
Claverdon
To Henley-in-Arden
North Jc.
West Jc. Bearley
Wilmcote
Birmingham Rd.
Stratford upon Avon S & M Jc.
Evesham Rd. Crossing H.
Old Town
To Broom
Race Course Chambers Crossing H.
To Kineton
Milcote
Long Marston
Pebworth H. Broad Marston H.
To Worcester
East Jc.
Honeybourne
South Jc.
Weston-sub-Edge
West Jc.
Willersey H.
To Oxford
Broadway
Laverton H.
Toddington
Gretton H.
Gotherington
Hayles
Abbey H.
Winchcombe
Bishop's
Race Course Cleeve
To Birmingham
High St. H.
Lansdown
St. James
Lansdown Jc.
Malvern Rd.
Cheltenham
To Gloucester
To Kingham
Andoversford
Hatherley Jc. Gloucester Loop Jc.
To Cirencester

N

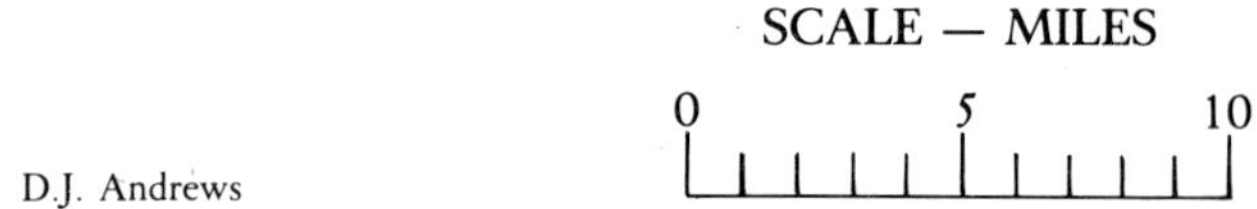

SCALE — MILES

0   5   10

D.J. Andrews

Introduction

Most of the privately preserved railways in Britain are, as originally built, single track lines, but the Gloucestershire Warwickshire Railway, giving a new significance to the initials GWR, is a line with a difference. It aims to restore the route from Cheltenham to Stratford upon Avon, a former double-track main line, and furthermore, one of the last to be built in England.

For many years critics of the Great Western Railway had claimed that its initials stood for 'Great Way Round' and certainly some of its routes were far from being bee-lines. Then around the turn of the century, the GWR began building cut-offs such as the Edington line shortening the route to Weymouth in 1900; the Bristol & South Wales Direct in 1903, the Honeybourne to Cheltenham line being a further example. A new railway was built from south of Birmingham to north of Stratford upon Avon, the existing Stratford to Honeybourne branch doubled and the line extended from Honeybourne to Cheltenham, making a direct route from Birmingham to Bristol as the GWR already possessed running powers over the Midland Railway from Standish. This new Honeybourne line formed a rival to the parallel Midland route from Birmingham to Gloucester.

The most famous train to traverse the Cheltenham—Stratford upon Avon line was 'The Cornishman', on its journey from Wolverhampton to Penzance. Here, No. 5026 "Criccieth Castle" is shown on a 'Down' working near Gotherington (minus headboard) on 2nd September 1962.

(W. Potter)

Although officially closed on 25th March 1968, Cheltenham Race Course station was used again for race trains in 1971. For this the old platform edging stones were lifted on the 'Up' platform which was resurfaced with gravel as can be seen here on 18th March that year. A 6-car d.m.u. waits at this platform having just arrived from Bristol. (W. Potter)

Collett designed 2884 class 2-8-0 No. 2887 passes Southam on a 'Down' goods, 11th June 1963. (W. Potter)

Opening of the Honeybourne to Stratford upon Avon Line

The Oxford, Worcester & Wolverhampton Railway, whose initials gave rise to the nickname, the Old Worse & Worse, obtained powers on 27th July 1846 to build a 9½ mile long standard gauge branch from Honeybourne on its main line, to Stratford upon Avon. The construction of this branch proved a long-winded affair. On 2nd August 1848 a Commissioner's of Railways' Warrant under Seal granted an extension of time, but this turned out to be quite insufficient and two further Acts had to be sought before it eventually opened to traffic on 12th July 1859. The line was constructed by the OWW using direct labour, a contractor not being employed as was customary.

Captain George Ross on behalf of the Board of Trade, inspected the completed line on 8th July 1859 finding a single line laid on sufficient land purchased for double line. The branch had been tested by 'heavy goods engines' belonging to the OWW, running over it for many weeks while carrying spoil to form the embankments and hauling ballast. Ross pointed out to John Fowler, the OWW's engineer, that the permanent way needed modification. The 18lb bracket chairs had been secured to the transverse sleepers by 6 inch wrought iron spikes. Ross said that within six weeks, the spikes at the sleepers adjacent to the joints should be replaced by fang bolts. Ross regretted that no telegraph had been installed. Despite these criticisms, he recommended that the branch be opened and in order to avoid head-on collisions on the single line, it be worked on the one-engine-in-steam principle. The Stratford terminus was temporary as the company had powers under its Act to extend the line to the railway's canal which separated the Honeybourne from the Hatton branch. The OWW did not propose approaching the canal more closely until the question of crossing it was settled with reference to the relative levels of the two branches.

The following year, on 1st July 1860, the OWW absorbed the Newport, Abergavenny & Hereford and the Worcester & Hereford Railway companies, the enlarged concern becoming the West Midland Railway, the latter company constructing a short connection with the Stratford upon Avon Railway.

Subsequent to the opening of the Honeybourne to Cheltenham line, the Honeybourne to Stratford branch was doubled and the sharper curves eased to allow fast running, Honeybourne East Junction to Long Marston being opened 28th April 1907, (the opportunity having been taken of easing the gradient from 1 in 130 to 1 in 150); Long Marston to Milcote 3rd March 1907 and Milcote to Stratford upon Avon East & West Junction on 9th February 1908. The line from East & West Junction to Slottery Footpath signal box had been doubled circa September 1899 and that from Slottery Footpath signal box to Stratford station in May 1902.

The Stratford upon Avon Railway

On 10th August 1857 the nominally independent Stratford upon Avon Railway was authorised to construct a 9¼ mile long single track mixed gauge line from a junction with the GWR's Birmingham to London main line at Hatton, to a terminus at Birmingham Road, Stratford, the line being opened 9th October 1860. To facilitate through traffic, the Stratford upon Avon Railway was authorised to construct a 29 chain connection to the branch from Honeybourne, this section being brought into use on 24th July 1861 for excursions to Warwick, a regular standard gauge passenger service commencing between Leamington, Worcester and Malvern on 1st August 1861 using the new connection. Birmingham Road station was closed to regular passenger traffic on 1st January 1863, but continued in use for excursions and freight. From this date all regular trains on the branch from Hatton were worked only on the standard gauge, although the broad gauge rail remained in situ for another six years. The Stratford upon Avon Railway was amalgamated with the GWR under an Act of 1st July 1883.

Birmingham, North Warwickshire & Stratford upon Avon Railway

In 1892 enthusiasm was shown for a proposed direct railway from Stratford upon Avon to Birmingham passing through Henley in Arden which at that time was four miles from a station. The Midland Railway was approached, but declined to consider the proposal, while the Great Western suggestion of building a branch from a junction with the GWR outside Birmingham to the Hatton to Stratford branch at Bearley was not met with local enthusiasm, especially as there was little hope of the GWR itself constructing the line. Then in 1894 a bill was introduced into Parliament backed by almost all the landowners, for an independent line over 24 miles in length running from the centre of Birmingham to Stratford. It was keenly contested in the Commons by both the Midland and Great Western, but the opposition of the former was withdrawn before the bill went to the Lords. During its course through Parliament, the Henley in Arden Railway from Rowington Junction was opened for traffic on 6th June 1894, 33 years after it had first been authorised. It was worked by the GWR. At Hatton where the Stratford branch joined the main line, the junction faced London, preventing a through service being run from Birmingham, which to some extent, would have obviated the BNWR threat; so in order to allow a Birmingham to Stratford service to operate, the GWR laid the North Curve, brought into use on 1st July 1897 and a fast train was put on from Birmingham, speeding the trip from an hour or more, to 43 minutes.

The GWR's opposition to the BNWR was because the promoters of the line had realised the great possibilities of their railway becoming part of a route from Birmingham to London only three miles longer than that of the London & North Western Railway and 16 miles shorter than the Great Western's route. A short spur at Stratford could have linked the BNWR with the East & West Junction Railway which would have been most willing to grant running powers over its line to the Great Central Railway then being built and which would have given access to London. The GWR countered this very real threat by promising the Lords' Committee that if the BNWR bill were rejected, the GWR would construct a line from Tyseley to either Bearley or Henley in Arden. Despite this promise, the BNWR received its Act on 25th August 1894. Unfortunately for the BNWR the Great Central withdrew its support and formed an alliance with the GWR.

Meanwhile south of Stratford, between Honeybourne, Broadway and Winchcombe, traders and fruit growers were pressing for a railway to serve the district. On 16th July 1866 an Act of Parliament had been granted to construct a line from near Beckford, on the Midland Railway's Ashchurch to Evesham branch, to Winchcombe, but the scheme had proved abortive. In 1898 a line was promoted to run from Stratford to the Midland & South Western Junction line at Andoversford. Seeing possibilities of access to Birmingham, the MSWJR proposed to work both the Andoversford & Stratford and the BNWR. As this scheme provided an alternative through route from Birmingham to Southampton, it naturally encountered strong opposition from both the MR and the GWR as traffic would have been diverted from their lines, the latter going so far as to pledge itself to construct a line from Honeybourne to Cheltenham if the bill were thrown out, which it was. This resulted in the BNWR finding it impossible to raise capital for construction and so made overtures to the GWR. By an Act of 9th August 1899 it abandoned the independent entry into Birmingham and instead, satisfied itself with a line from the GWR at Tyseley to the Stratford branch at Bearley, these powers being taken over by the GWR in an Act of 30th July 1900.

Because the GWR was engaged in so much construction elsewhere and funds were thus taken up, it was not until 5th September 1905 that C.J. Wills & Sons started work on the contract. The BNWR opened to goods traffic 9th December 1907, while passenger trains, including an express from Wolverhampton to Bristol and back, started on 1st July 1908. From Bearley West Junction to Honeybourne the original single line was doubled and the gradients reduced in places to render the line more suitable for express trains. At Stratford upon Avon a sharp curve north of the station was eased.

The Cheltenham to Honeybourne Line

Bristol and Birmingham were both key divisions on the Great Western, but in the eighteen-nineties there was no direct link between them. They were however joined by the Midland Railway's main line, the direct distance being 88¾ miles, or 91¼ miles via Worcester. These distances were very advantageous compared with the GWR routes of 132½ miles via Smethwick Junction, Worcester, Hereford, Pontypool Road and the Severn Tunnel, or 140 miles via Oxford, Didcot and Bath. Therefore it was not surprising that the lion's share of the local traffic from Bristol to Birmingham and vice versa, or a large proportion of that emanating from places on the Great Western system further afield, when it converged on Bristol or Birmingham, was transferred to Midland trains. The primary object of the Great Western creating a new route was to enable it to compete on an equal level, the GWR particularly desirous of retaining passengers from beyond Bristol or Birmingham by removing the temptation to change systems.

The matter was brought to a head in 1898 when the independent Midland & South Western Junction Railway supported the Andoversford & Stratford Railway as mentioned above. Because this was a threat to what the GWR considered its territory, Lord Cawdor, chairman of the GWR, secured the bill's rejection on the undertaking that his company would forthwith proceed with a line from Cheltenham to Honeybourne, which, with the existing branch thence to Stratford, was expected to serve the district better than one from Andoversford. Thus on 1st August 1899, Parliamentary powers were granted for the GWR to construct a line from Cheltenham to Honeybourne; double the branch from Honeybourne through Stratford to Bearley where a loop was to connect with the BNWR, which, as recorded above, was in the same session of Parliament.

The GWR was able to create a new route from Birmingham to Bristol without constructing a new line 90 miles in length because part of the route was already in existence, either belonging to the GWR, or being lines over which the company had running powers. Apart from the BNWR from Tyseley to Bearley, the only completely new line needed was that bridging the 20¾ mile gap between Cheltenham and Honeybourne. The GWR possessed running powers over the Midland Railway between Bristol and Gloucester via Mangotsfield and Berkeley Road. This was because the line was originally built by an independent company in which the GWR had obtained a controlling interest, with the result that it was first of all laid to the broad gauge. Now at the same period, the GWR was also backing the Cheltenham & Great Western Union Railway which started from Swindon. To save on construction costs, these two broad gauge lines made a junction at Standish and used a joint line onwards to Gloucester and Cheltenham. In 1845 the Bristol & Gloucester amalgamated with the Birmingham & Gloucester, the latter being a standard gauge line and a year later the joint undertakings were invested in the Midland Railway, subject to the proviso in the Bristol & Birmingham and Midland Railway's Act of 1846 that the latter should 'at all times hereafter maintain in the line from Bristol to Standish Junction, two lines of railway on the same gauge as the Great Western Railway' and permit GWR trains to 'pass at all reasonable and proper times'. In 1848 the MR obtained powers to construct a new standard gauge railway between Gloucester and Standish Junction and to lay a third rail to accommodate standard gauge trains between Standish and Bristol. On 1st August 1871 the GWR ran its Gloucester to Bristol goods trains over the MR line, but discontinued the service after the opening of the Severn Tunnel route on 1st September 1886.

The line between Gloucester and Cheltenham was the joint property of the GWR and MR, the former having inherited it from the Cheltenham & Great Western Union Railway and the latter from the Birmingham & Gloucester. The CGWUR owned the line between Cheltenham and Churchdown situated midway between Cheltenham and Gloucester, and the Birmingham & Gloucester owned the remaining section from Churchdown to Gloucester. The line was laid with mixed gauge so that trains of both companies could use it. To ensure strict impartiality in working the line, the two companies had entered into a curious arrangement whereby each appointed the other trustee for the section which it owned, the trains of both companies using the whole line without paying rent or toll to one another. The old Gloucester 'Avoiding Line' of 1847 was re-opened on 25th November 1901 for goods traffic. As GWR through trains from Bristol to Cheltenham would have had to reverse if using the GWR station at Gloucester which was situated on the South Wales line, it was intended that a new station called Gloucester, Chequers Bridge, would be erected at a cost of £30,000 at the southern end of the loop, though in the event, this was never constructed because of a contention with Gloucester City Corporation over access.

The contractors for the Cheltenham and Honeybourne line, Messrs Walter Scott & Middleton, started work at Honeybourne towards the end of 1902, hutted accommodation for navvies being provided at Toddington and Gretton. A year later, an unusual accident occurred at Stanway Viaduct between Laverton and Toddington. For some weeks, gangs of 30 to 40 men had been engaged in working day and night shifts building the viaduct. At 8.15 am on Friday 13th November 1903 three arches collapsed out of the ten then completed. At the time, about twenty men were engaged in removing the false arches from the completed spans which then fell. Of these men, two were killed on the spot and two died subsequently, while seven others were more or less seriously injured and were conveyed to the Winchcombe Cottage Hospital and Winchcombe Workhouse Hospital where "medical attention was promptly given." The contractors had sufficient social conscience to compensate the families of the men killed. Frederick Gibbins was killed by the crane falling on him. He was really a pork butcher, but not having been successful in business, was making ends meet by undertaking general labouring work.

The arches fell in the reverse order of construction, No.10 being the first to collapse. When No.10 fell, the adjoining arches on the north side having lost their support, followed; No.9 falling ten minutes after, and No.8 twenty minutes later. No.7 fell next day and by this time the contractors had managed to secure the others by binding together the whole of the finished arches which still remained with steel chains and in addition, placed huge timber baulks as supports to the one which had shown movement—that is, the one adjacent to that which had last fallen. Construction of arch No.10 had been begun on 6th October and completed on 29th October. Five sets of centreing were used on the viaduct which C.T. Scott, the director immediately in charge, said was 'extravagant', three sets having been used by some other contractors undertaking similar work.

The disaster was caused by the five centres being removed before the hydraulic lime mortar joining the brickwork had set. The mortar consisted of one part of Warwickshire blue lias lime, one part sand and one part furnace ashes. The arches were of five courses, making a total thickness of 1ft 10½ins. The steam crane working on top of No.10 arch at the time of the disaster and engaged on lifting out the wooden centreing for use in No.15 arch, (the last one), hastened the catastrophe and increased its effect. The weight of the crane was spread along heavy timber beams 54ft long by 18ins square, the weight of the crane being 13 tons plus the wooden rib it was lifting, this amounting to 1 ton 12 cwt. A verdict of accidental

The 15 arch, Stanway Viaduct near Toddington during its construction in 1904. Note the contractor's temporary track at ground level.
(C.G. Magg's collection)

Stanway Viaduct, just north of Toddington, following the collapse of four of the ten arches then completed. Three arches fell on 13th November 1903 with another on the next day. This resulted in the death of four men, plus injury to seven others, but this was the only serious accident to occur during the construction of the railway. *(C.G. Magg's collection)*

death was brought in, a rider being added that insufficient time was given for the lime mortar to set before the centres were removed; that similar arches should have cement mortar and that the steam crane had been carried further on to No.10 arch than was advisable. The arches were rebuilt using cement mortar.

The line from Honeybourne to Broadway, together with the spur from Honeybourne North signal box to West Loop Box was inspected by Colonel H. Arthur Yorke. He found all the works substantially built, the girders under the lines giving very moderate deflections when tested with heavy engines. A certificate was granted, the railway being opened on 1st August 1904. In November he inspected the section to Toddington. Two embankments showed signs of settlement and he ordered that a watch be kept on them and that speed be restricted to 10 mph. He found Stanway Viaduct perfectly sound. The steam railmotor service was extended to Toddington on 1st December. Goods trains had worked to the station since 1st August, but passenger trains could not be operated as the passenger station was incomplete.

On 26th January 1905 Colonel Yorke inspected the section to Winchcombe, only one platform being brought into use when the line was opened on 1st February 1905. The first train arrived at Winchcombe at 7.18 am and left at 7.24. 68 passengers bought tickets, mostly to Toddington. As 17 passengers had arrived on the first train holding return tickets, 85 went out on the 7.24 which consisted of one motor car and trailer. The ten trains that day were all well-patronised. The connection onwards to Cheltenham was by GWR motor bus. A trial trip had been run on 31st January using GWR bus No.11, AF 74 on the Cornwall County register, for it had run on the Great Western's Helston to the Lizard route before coming to Gloucestershire. Its body was of light brown wood with seats for 18 passengers inside the saloon and two outside beside the driver, luggage accommodation being on the roof. The interior of the saloon was lit by an acetylene lamp. The body was on a Milnes-Daimler chassis powered by a 20-24 hp engine with 4-speed gear box. It was capable of a maximum speed of 30 mph on its solid rubber tyres, twin on the rear axle, though in practice, a steady 10 mph was maintained, the timetable allowing one hour twenty minutes for the ten mile run via Bishop's Cleeve. It departed from St. James' station yard at 2.30 pm, arriving at Winchcombe station at 3.33 where it was housed in a temporary shed in the station yard. Two buses ran a service of three trips each way daily. On 30th May 1906, Colonel Yorke inspected the line to Bishop's Cleeve, it being opened on 1st June and the bus service to Winchcombe was cut back to Bishop's Cleeve.

On 19th May, Scott & Middleton's 0-6-0 saddle tank engine *Pallion* had hauled five contractors' open wagons containing members of the Gloucestershire Engineering Society on a return trip from Cheltenham to Winchcombe. On 23rd July, G.W. Blackhall, divisional engineer to the GWR, ran his inspection saloon over the line from Cheltenham to Bishop's Cleeve. On 26th July, Colonel Yorke carried out the Board of Trade inspection, the line being opened on 1st August 1906, three months ahead of schedule. A temporary station was used at Malvern Road, Cheltenham, until a permanent structure was opened on 30th March 1908.

The scene at Broadway station on 1st August 1904, the day the line was opened from Honeybourne as far as this point.
(John Jacques courtesy H.L. Blinkhorn)

GWR bus No. 11 at Winchcombe station on 31st January 1905. The bus service was operated linking first Winchcombe, and later Bishop's Cleeve with Cheltenham, St. James' station as the railway was progressively extended southwards. *(C.G. Magg's collection)*

Manning Wardle 1525 "Pallion", 0-6-0ST worked a special train from Cheltenham to Winchcombe on 19th May 1906 for the benefit of members of the Gloucestershire Engineering Society. *(C.G. Magg's collection)*

Members of the Gloucestershire Engineering Society in contractor's wagon No. 135 on the occasion of their visit to the railway, 19th May 1906. They travelled from Cheltenham to Winchcombe prior to the official opening of this section. (C.G. Magg's collection)

The Board of Trade inspection train at Gotherington station on 26th July 1906.
(Courtesy 'The Engineer')

A steam railmotor on a 'Down' service at Bishop's Cleeve c1910.   *(Lens of Sutton)*

The line from Honeybourne had cost about £½m and gave employment to 1,200 men, there being no serious accident except that at Stanway Viaduct. James C. Inglis was engineer when Parliamentary powers were obtained; the line was located by G.W. Blackhall, Divisional Engineer, Gloucester; Walter Armstrong was the New Works Engineer and prepared the contract carried out under J.C. Blundell, Resident Engineer, assisted by Mr. Stanley and R.B. Blackhall. The contractors were represented by C.T. Scott, assisted by J.E. Chapman as Chief Engineer and Mr. Avery as Second Engineer. For the construction of the line, the GWR supplied the contractors with rails (97½ lb per yard); chairs (52 lb each); sleepers; crushed slag ballasting and also white stone chippings for roads in yards and station approaches; iron railings for stations; standard GWR creosoted posts and eight-wire fencing.

The old single track from Honeybourne to Stratford upon Avon was doubled by Messrs Walter Scott & Middleton, the stations at Milcote and Long Marston being rebuilt. The heaviest work was the building of a new viaduct over the Avon near Stratford. The railway became a main line when a service of express passenger trains began on 1st July 1908 from Birmingham to Bristol, the fastest train covering the distance of 98 miles in two hours thirty five minutes.

The line developed its anticipated potential in providing a direct Great Western route from Birmingham to Bristol and the West of England, and also to South Wales, while apart from through trains, it generated a fair amount of local traffic, particularly during the fruit season. In the British Railways era it still continued to provide an alternative to the former Midland Railway's Gloucester to Birmingham

LMSR 8F class 2-8-0 No. 8469 heads an iron ore train through Bishops's Cleeve in April 1945 having been completed at the GWR's Swindon Works the previous month. *(W. Potter)*

route up the Lickey Incline. In 1964 the Lickey Incline carried 90,000 tons of freight weekly; the Worcester and Hereford line 70,000 tons and Honeybourne to Cheltenham 60,000 tons. Between 2nd February and 6th April 1958 the line was closed to enable blanketing to be carried out at Weston sub Edge, trains being diverted via Honeybourne, Evesham and the Midland branch to Ashchurch, regaining their normal route at Lansdown Junction, Cheltenham.

The Cheltenham to Honeybourne local passenger service was withdrawn on 7th March 1960, though some stations remained open for parcels traffic and Cheltenham Racecourse station continued in use for race meetings until 21st March 1968. When this closed, the line was still maintained up to passenger standard so that it could be used as a diversionary route. From 4th June 1951 a number of heavy freight and iron ore trains between the former Great Central Railway and South Wales were diverted from the route via Banbury and Swindon, to the Stratford upon Avon and Midland Junction Railway at Woodford West Junction, then by the south curve at Broom Junction to the Midland line at Ashchurch. Later, the authorities decided to shorten the route by making a new junction at Stratford to allow through running towards Honeybourne. This junction, south of the Racecourse station was put in on 24th April 1960, principally because by this time, part of the Banbury & Cheltenham Railway had been closed. The junction was first used on 12th June 1960, but was destined to enjoy only a short life, for on 1st January 1963 the boundary between the Western Region and the London Midland Region was redrawn from the London—Banbury—Birmingham route, the new line of demarcation lying just south of Racecourse Junction. Steadily the local traffic dwindled and trains were confined to steel traffic to and from South Wales and ironstone trains. Coupled with this, geographical difficulties prevented full exploitation of the ironstone mines, and together with the elimination of the Great Central main line and the traffic it generated, Racecourse Junction was closed on 1st March 1965, most of the SMJR closing shortly after on 5th July. With the closure of Racecourse Junction, Woodford to South Wales trains were re-routed via Washwood Heath and the Lickey Incline and the dwindling iron ore traffic from Banbury, together with most of the inter-regional freight, was dieselised and diverted via Didcot by 8th November 1965. Back in September 1960 loadings of the North East to South Wales steel trains had been tested by a dynamometer car being included in trains from Woodford Halse to Honeybourne over a period of three days. War Department type 2-8-0s Nos.90448, 90638 and 90237 being the train engines. It was discovered that loads could be increased to 800 tons.

After the diversion of most inter-regional traffic by 8th November 1965, the only regular traffic over the line between Cheltenham and Stratford were three freight and two parcels trains; the former were diverted leaving only the parcels trains, which were withdrawn from 6th March 1967. The line was again used regularly for freight from the beginning of May 1970.

On 25th August 1976, 22 wagons of the 06.35 hr Toton to Severn Tunnel Junction coal train became derailed at Winchcombe damaging the track. Although the 'Up' line was brought into use for special brake test trains by the Railway Technical Centre, Derby between Greet and Gotherington during September and October, it was considered uneconomic to repair the 'Down' line and both tracks of the Cheltenham to Honeybourne line were officially closed on 1st November 1976. The line from Honeybourne to Long Marston was retained as a single track, long siding.

Description of the Line from Cheltenham to Stratford upon Avon

The Honeybourne line left the Midland route to Birmingham at Lansdown Junction, south of the MR's Cheltenham Lansdown station, the junction being sited at the northern apex of a triangular junction made by the Banbury & Cheltenham Railway. Since closure of the Honeybourne line, the main line curve has been realigned. Cheltenham Malvern Road station (0 miles 50 chains) was opened on 30th March 1908 to deal with through trains to and from Honeybourne, thus obviating the need for a reversal into St. James' terminus. Malvern Road had a slightly curved island platform 700 feet in length, reached over a footbridge from the booking office, the verandah and footbridge largely constructed of Universal Roof Covering supplied by Messrs S. Taylor & Co. Steam railmotors reversed in the bay platform at the 'Up' end of the station on their way to or from St. James' but when replaced by auto trains hauled by tank engines, this bay was generally not

The 'Honeybourne Line' joined the Midland route from Birmingham at Lansdown Junction, Cheltenham. No. 6814 "Enborne Grange" brings a goods train under Lansdown Road bridge, heading south on 8th June 1963. (J. Wood)

long enough and the down platform was used. As a wartime economy measure, the station was closed from 1st January 1917 to 7th July 1919. On 1st February 1925 'Spa' was added to the name. The station, which came under the supervision of the St. James' stationmaster, closed to goods and passengers 3rd January 1966. North of the station was Malvern Road Junction (0.69 miles) where the Honeybourne line and the branch to St. James' station bifurcated, trains at this point being subject to a speed limit of 25 mph. The direction from Cheltenham to Honeybourne is designated 'Up'.

The construction of the first three quarters of a mile of line involved the acquisition and demolition of about 70 cottages in Great Western Road, Bloomsbury Place, Carlton Place, Hill View Cottages, Marsh Cottages and Whitehart Street, the latter being crossed diagonally and made into a cul de sac. The Cherry Tree Inn was also demolished. The GWR was required by law to provide accommodation for those dispossessed of their homes, the company only having to provide for those whose work was within a mile of the cottages demolished; a laundress whose work was at Charlton Kings two miles away, failed to come within the scheme. Compensating houses were built by the GWR in Sandfield Road on Grange Court estate. The construction of the new line involved cutting off a corner of the Old Cemetery and the removal of 300 bodies interred there. In the first half mile there were no less than seven large bridges; under St. George's Road, and over the River Chelt, Millbrook Street, Market Street, High Street, Swindon Road and St. Paul's Road.

High Street halt (1.19 miles) was opened 1st October 1908 but was closed 30th April 1917 as a wartime economy measure. The line fell for half a mile at 1 in 116 to a point prior to Hunting Butts tunnel, 79 yards in length and lined with seven courses of blue Staffordshire bricks making a total thickness of 2ft 7½ins. This tunnel, together with its considerable approach cuttings, required an excavation of almost 220,000 cu yards of spoil. Cheltenham Racecourse station (2.69 miles) opened for race meetings starting 13th March 1912. It was provided with strong barriers to guard against the crush and allowed passengers to come out only in three streams, thus making life difficult for fare dodgers. The signal box was only opened on race days. The shelters and toilets on both platforms were removed about 1963. The station was officially closed on 25th March 1968, having last been used on the 21st for the Gold Cup meeting. However it was used again for race course traffic in 1971, for which the platforms were resurfaced. The line curved northwards to avoid the heights of Cleeve Common and the expense of a 4,000 yard tunnel below it.

The covered footbridge connecting the booking office with the island platform at Malvern Road station, 9th October 1965. (C.G. Maggs) Station exterior. (L.B. Lapper)

Above: 'Black Five' 4-6-0 No. 45006 pauses at Malvern Road station to receive water whilst en route from Ilfracombe and Minehead to Wolverhampton, 28th August 1965.   (W. Potter)

Left: Cheltenham Spa Malvern Road West Signal Box, 27th April 1933.   (P. Copeland)

Below: 3-car d.m.u. forming the 11.02 Gloucester Central—Cheltenham St. James' passes Malvern Road station on 9th October 1965. (C.G. Maggs)

The vast area of track through Malvern Road station can be seen in this photograph, taken on 10th July 1946. The slight curve of the 700ft platform is also shown. (L.E. Copeland)

A general view of Cheltenham Spa (Malvern Road) on 30th July 1965, with 0-6-0 pannier tank No. 8745 on the 17.00 hrs Gloucester Central—Cheltenham St. James' service. The locomotive coaling stage/water tank can be seen on the right. (W. Potter)

View from St. George's Road bridge during construction of the line through Cheltenham in February 1906. Note the contractor's narrow gauge line worked by horse traction.

(C.G. Magg's collection)

The boring of the 79 yard long Hunting Butts tunnel in 1906.   *(C.G. Magg's collection)*

Hunting Butts tunnel viewed from the south, 19th April 1968.   *(C.G. Maggs)*

The road level ticket office of Cheltenham Race Course station, April 1968. This building survives today although currently in urgent need of renovation.   *(C.G. Maggs)*

Cheltenham Race Course station, looking north.   *(Lens of Sutton)*

Below: Class 52 C-C diesel hydraulic D1061 "Western Envoy" on a first class only race special ex London, Paddington at Cheltenham Race Course station, 6th March 1964.   *(W. Potter)*

Bishop's Cleeve station on 5th March 1960, the last day of passenger services to local stations. 0-6-0 pannier tank No. 8488 works a single coach train from Honeybourne to Cheltenham.   (W. Potter)

Bishop's Cleeve (4.56 miles) was built of Cleeve Hill stone with pea-grip quoins and plinths, while the platform copings were of stone brought from Pontypridd. A heavy crane was provided in the station yard for dealing with stone traffic. The station, like the others on the line, was equipped with a goods shed and cattle pens. The signal box was of standard Great Western design, but built of stone rather than the usual timber or brick; it had 22 levers in use and 9 spare. The station was used for stabling race specials. For instance in 1930 when the National Hunt Steeplechase meeting took place, all the sidings were cleared of wagons so that they

Single car diesel unit, No. M55004 passing through Bishop's Cleeve station on 4th September 1965, by which time the platforms had been removed.   (W. Potter)

'Britannia' class 4-6-2 No. 70045 "Lord Rowallan" storms through Bishop's Cleeve with a Saturday special from the South Coast to Birmingham Snow Hill and Wolverhampton, 4th September 1965. On the right is the old goods shed, with the tracks removed. (W. Potter)

B.R. Standard 9F class 2-10-0 No. 92152 passes Bishop's Cleeve goods shed with an 'Up' freight on 27th July 1963. This goods yard had only just become disused, having been closed on the 1st of the month. (W. Potter)

Gotherington station looking in the 'Up' direction, showing the station as it was in the 1930's. (D. Thompson)

could be used for the specials headed by two and four cylinder 4-6-0s, ready to go forward to the Racecourse station after the meeting. Racehorses were unloaded at Bishop's Cleeve and walked along the main road to the course. As at many of the stations on this line, the front siding between the goods shed road and the main line could be used as a refuge siding, the points being normally locked towards the front siding. Following closure of the goods yard on 1st July 1963, race trains were stabled in the yard at St. James'. Beyond the station, the gradient steepened to 1 in 150 rising to Gotherington (6.19 miles) which also had a stone building. The two-road goods yard closed and the station became an unstaffed halt on 1st January 1941, though track in the yard was not taken out of use until the signal box with 20 levers plus 13 spare, closed on 3rd April 1949. The halt shut to passengers on 13th January 1955; it had been placed to serve the hamlets of Woolstone, Dixton and Prescott. The road beyond the station crossed at a very acute angle necessitating a heavy steel bridge. Not far beyond, the line entered the 60ft deep, steep-sided Dixton cutting from which 115,000 cu yards of spoil were excavated. Then followed an embankment 30ft high and almost a mile in length containing 250,000 cu yds.

Three quarters of a mile beyond Gretton halt (8.16 miles) with 100ft long platforms, is Greet Tunnel, 693 yards in length. This tunnel was speedily built — the first 18ft of brickwork being completed on 7th November 1904 and the last on 5th December 1905, two shafts being used to expedite the work. The tunnel was cut through blue lias, the excavation of which required a considerable use of explosives, the clay proving to be harder than many rocks. Making the tunnel and its approach cuttings involved the shifting of 370,000 cu yds of material. Similar to Hunting Butts tunnel, it has a seven course brick lining, recesses on alternate sides

South portal of the 693 yard long Greet Tunnel, April 1968.   *(C.G. Maggs)*

being provided for platelayers at intervals of 22yds. The tunnel, 297ft above the Ordnance datum, marks the summit of the line. The railway undulates, but gradually falls towards Milcote. It descends in a semi-circle to approach as near as possible to Winchcombe and yet avoid the high ground. Winchcombe (9.52 miles), like the remaining stations on the line to Honeybourne, was built of red brick on a plinth of blue brick. Its platforms were 400ft in length. Unusually for the GWR, the station nameboard at the 'Down' end of the 'Up' platform was set at an angle of 45° to the track. This was probably due to the fact that the platform was on a left hand curve. The station was exactly a mile from the town centre. The station had a commodious goods shed in the extensive goods yard, closed 2nd November 1964. Traffic returns for 1913 were:

> Number of passengers: 21,824
> Fares collected: £1,436
> Coal and coke: 5,517 tons
> Livestock — forwarded: 170 wagons
>   — received: 54 wagons
> Total receipts, goods and passengers: £5,837

A 2251 class 0-6-0 heads an 'Up' goods through Winchcombe in 1960. Note the station nameboard which is angled at 45° to the track.   *(P.J. Garland)*

Looking in the 'Up' direction along the platform at Winchcombe, towards the goods shed and signal box.   *(Lens of Sutton)*

The signal box had 24 levers in use and 7 spares. The contractors found that the blue clay forming the embankments failed to hold its shape unless free from moisture. To overcome this problem, adjacent to the bridge over the A46 road the contractors dug trenches 30—60 feet apart down to the original ground level, bracing the sides with strong timbering. These trenches were filled with slag and the timbers gradually drawn out. The clay clung to the slag and kept its shape, while the water was able to drain away through the material. Hayles Abbey halt (11.14 miles) with its sleeper-edged platform and corrugated iron shelters, opened 24th September 1928.

A 'Down' view of Winchcombe station 7th June 1954.   *(L.B. Lapper)*

Hayles Abbey halt looking towards Toddington in the 1960's.　　　　　　　　*(P.J. Garland)*

Toddington station (12.16 miles) was built as a large receiving centre for fruit, the goods yard having a fruit shed in addition to a goods shed. At the height of the fruit season, 70—80 trucks were loaded and sent away daily. At the turn of the century, Lord Sudeley planned a scheme which proved abortive, for an electrically powered light railway to connect his orchards and jam factory at Toddington with the Midland Railway's Ashchurch to Evesham branch at Beckford. About the same period he actually built a narrow gauge tramway half a mile in length, with branches serving his orchards (SP 045325), while some twenty years later the Timber Supply Department of the Board of Trade operated a 600mm gauge line with an 0-4-0 petrol locomotive, Baguley Cars Ltd, Works No.776, built 1919 to McEwan Pratt design.

Toddington looking south, to Cheltenham in the peaceful days of the 1960's. This site is now the scene of intense activity being the centre of operations for the new G.W.R.—the Gloucestershire Warwickshire Railway.

　　　　　　　　(P.J. Garland)

Toddington passenger station, like Broadway, was lit by acetylene gas. Water cranes were sited at the ends of the platforms. The station was the last to be closed to goods, this taking place on 2nd January 1967, a short length of the front siding being retained for use by engineers' trains. At the time of the line's closure in 1976, Toddington was the only intermediate signal box between Honeybourne West and Lansdown Junction. When the goods yard was open the box had 23 levers in use and 6 spare. Beyond the station the line fell for three quarters of a mile at 1 in 150. The line crossed the 630ft long Stanway Viaduct with 15 arches of 36ft span, and a maximum height of 42ft. Its foundations and abutments were constructed in Warwickshire blue lias lime concrete, the remainder being brickwork in lime mortar. The arches are in Staffordshire brindle bricks, the remainder of the work being of wire-cut bricks faced with brindles. The clay in the embankments at either end was stabilised by being burnt until dry. A mile or so south of Laverton, a stream had to be carried across the cutting in a box trough, which doubled as a footbridge.

Laverton (14.49 miles) was a simple rail motor halt opened on 14th August 1905, and built of timber like the other halts on the line. It served Laverton, Buckland, Wormington and Stanton. Approaching Broadway, was the heaviest embankment on the line, a mile in length, it contained about 310,000 cu yds of material. It was on fire in several places for years, defying efforts with sand and cement to seal them off. The goods station at Broadway (16.59 miles) was rather interesting as it was built on 'made' ground. As the formation had not settled sufficiently to support the

Toddington, as it was in 1960, looking towards Honeybourne. The large water tank on the right, the footbridge and the platforms were subsequently removed but fortunately the station buildings have survived and are now being restored to their former glory. (P.J. Garland)

The state of Toddington station on 19th April 1968 with platforms removed. (C.G. Maggs)

An auto coach propelled by a tank locomotive at Toddington in the 1930's. A line of open wagons is visible in the goods yard, to the right of the footbridge. (D. Thompson)

The 15-arch Stanway Viaduct, 630 feet in length, to the north of Toddington is a spectacular feature on the line which should soon be in use again by steam hauled trains. Photographed in April 1968. (C.G. Maggs)

Pannier tank No.9727 arriving at Toddington with the 1.00 pm Cheltenham—Broadway train, 27th February 1960.   *(D.H. Ballantyne)*

brick wall of the usual type of shed, concrete pillars were built up from the original ground level and cast iron girders placed on them on which the brick shed could be built. The part of the passenger platform on the embankment was built of timber. The original temporary signal box contained 12 levers in use, 1 spare lever and a key for working the ground frame on the 'Down' side of the main line controlling the entrance to the goods yard, the frame being electrically controlled from the signal box. With the extension to Toddington, a new box was opened at Broadway with 28 levers in use and 9 spares. The ground frame had 6 levers all in use. The

Broadway station looking in the 'Up' direction c1904. The timber sections of the platforms can be seen here, these being built on the embankment which had not fully settled at this time.

(Photo: G.W.R.)

entrance from the 'Down' main line at the Toddington end of the yard was on a gradient of 1 in 50 and it was stipulated that 'the greatest care must be exercised by all concerned in shunting wagons into these sidings'. It was the duty of the guard to see that sufficient brakes were put down on wagons furthest from the engine to secure a proper control. The engine was required to remain attached to the wagons until they were brought to a stand in the sidings and a supply of sprags had to be kept on hand. The goods shed line and the front road were level with the main line. The signal box, closed 10th October 1960, was replaced by intermediate block signals, these being controlled from Toddington, Broadway ground frame also being electrically released from there.

Broadway closed to goods on 1st June 1964. The line descended at 1 in 200/150 through Willersey Halt (18.05 miles) to Bretforton & Weston-sub-Edge (19.34 miles), shortened to Weston-sub-Edge on 1st May 1907 and closed to goods 25th September 1950 on which date it became an unstaffed halt. Its signal box contained 20 levers in use and 7 spares. Half a mile beyond, the line crossed the Roman Icknield Street which necessitated 20,000 cu yds of material having to be tipped to carry the road over the line.

The Great Western gave thought regarding covering the scars to the environment caused by building the railway and landscaped many of the station sites with conifers. Lattice tops were fitted to the steel girder bridges giving them a much more attractive appearance than mere plain girders. As houses were scarce, three homes for permanent way staff were built at each of Bretforton, Broadway, Winchcombe, Gotherington and Bishop's Cleeve, while five were erected at Toddington. Immediately south of the Honeybourne Junctions, eight new sidings were brought

Willersey Halt provided the basic necessities for passengers—wooden platforms and the distinctive GWR pagoda style corrugated iron waiting shelters. Similar to this were Gretton and Laverton halts.
(L.B. Lapper)

Weston-sub-Edge—an early view with a steam railmotor train on a southbound working.
(Lens of Sutton)

into use in 1958, all being taken out of use on 27th July 1966, three being restored on 3rd November 1970. Just before passing under a girder bridge carrying the Oxford to Worcester line, the West loop gave access to Honeybourne Junction station (22.02 miles) and the engineer's tip. The two-road Honeybourne station on the Oxford to Worcester line, was enlarged to a four-track layout in 1909. Honeybourne's claim to fame, apart from being a junction, was that it was one of the first places in the country to have a signal box with an interlocking frame mechanically preventing conflicting signal and point levers from being pulled. The yard closed to goods 1st January 1964 and the station to passengers on 5th May 1969. As the village had doubled in size since the station closed and Long Lartin maximum security prison has been built a mile from the station, creating extra employment in the area, the station was re-opened on 22nd May 1981, being the

Honeybourne Junction station was served by local trains, to and from Stratford upon Avon and Cheltenham. A general view of the station in the early 1960's, looking in the 'Up' direction, towards Oxford.
(P.J. Garland)

Above: A period view of the island platform building and canopy at Honeybourne Junction.
(J.J. Herd collection)

Left: Mogul No. 6345 receives water at Honeybourne Junction station in 1963 whilst on an 'Up' goods train.
(P.J. Garland)

Below: An 0-4-2T with an auto train is prepared for departure from Honeybourne Junction.
(C.G. Magg's collection)

A platform level view of Pebworth Halt, looking 'Up'. (Lens of Sutton)

66th station to be opened or re-opened by BR since 1966. Honeybourne North loop closed 3rd November 1970, freight trains to Long Marston having to reverse at the West Loop, but in 1981 the line between Honeybourne and Honeybourne East Junction was reinstated as a single track, lines to the West loop being recovered late that year. At East Loop Junction (21.52 miles), the lines from Oxford and Worcester respectively, joined the line from Cheltenham. The line falls for three quarters of a mile at 1 in 142/111. Pebworth halt (22.53 miles), a sleeper built platform with wooden shelters, opened 6th September 1937 and closed, like the other stations on the Stratford branch, on the withdrawal of the stopping passenger

A view of Pebworth Halt from road level, March 1967 just after a year of closure, which had taken place on 3rd January 1966. (D.J. Hyde)

service on 3rd January 1966. Broad Marston Halt (22.69 miles) opened 17th October 1904 was closed 14th July 1916 as a wartime economy measure. Prior to reaching Long Marston there is quite an extensive nest of Ministry of Defence sidings, the Royal Engineers' Depot having its own timber-built platform. The sidings are worked by MoD locomotives. The MoD sidings had a truck weighbridge which was also available for BR use. There is also a large scrapyard at Long Marston belonging to Birds Commercial Metals Ltd, where many railway vehicles end their days, including London Transport underground stock. Long Marston station (24.09 miles) had on the 'Down' platform an attractive stone-built domestic style station building with unusually decorative barge boards. Until 1892 the platforms were staggered, but that year the 'Up' platform was moved northwards so that it was opposite the 'Down' which was lengthened. In 1936 the interlocking frame in the signal box, together with the level crossing stops, were renewed at a cost of £500. The station closed to goods 7th September 1964. The former single platform on the 'Down' side of the line at Milcote was closed 9th May 1908. The station building, similar but not identical to that at Long Marston remained, with new 400ft long platforms and Great Western style buildings replacing it north of the level crossing at 26.55 miles. The station was unstaffed from 1st March 1956 and closed to goods 1st July 1963. The signal box and lever frame are preserved in the Birmingham Railway Museum, Tyseley. A warning bell, activated and discontinued by trains passing over treadles, was provided for the safety of road users of the occupation level crossing at Pearce's Crossing 530yds north of Milcote station. Chambers Crossing Halt (27.11 miles) opened and closed on the same dates as Broad Marston. The River Avon was crossed by a viaduct 140 yards in length. It required replacement when the line was doubled in 1908. Consisting of nine brick spans for floodwater and a river span, the latter measured 114ft. The present structure replaced eight brick arches and two openings of 50ft spanned by wrought iron girders.

The Ministry of Defence timber built platform at Long Marston, June 1979. (C.G. Maggs)

The Ministry of Defence sidings at Long Marston in April 1968. The locomotive shed can be seen in the centre of the yard and the double track of the B.R. line to Stratford upon Avon on the left of the picture. The continued use of these sidings by the M.o.D., together with those of the adjoining scrap yard have ensured that the line from Honeybourne remains open to the present day.

(C.G. Maggs)

A commercial post card view of Long Marston station, prior to the erection of the footbridge. Note the very decorative barge boards on the domestic style station building.   *(Lens of Sutton)*

A more recent view of Long Marston, with footbridge installed.   (Lens of Sutton)

The original Milcote station buildings and signal box, 19th April 1968. This single platform station was closed 9th May 1908 and replaced by another to the north of the level crossing.
(C.G. Maggs)

The replacement Milcote station of 1908, with its 400ft long platforms and more typical GWR style buildings. Photographed 19th April 1968. (C.G. Maggs)

The S.L.S. special train of 24th April 1965 at Stratford upon Avon Race Course Platform. The locomotive is an 0-6-0 pannier tank, No. 6435 restored to GWR livery. (W. Potter)

Half a mile beyond the viaduct was Racecourse Junction where a curve opened 24th April 1960 and led to Old Town station, Stratford. On the original line was Stratford Racecourse station (28.68 miles), opened 6th May 1933, the platforms being 550ft in length, the platform facing consisting of sleepers supported by Barlow rail. The line passed below the single Stratford & Midland Junction Railway. At Stratford & Midland Junction signal box (29.11 miles) the other spur from Old Town station came in. Evesham Road Crossing halt (29.18 miles) opened 17th October 1904 and closed 14th July 1916. North of the crossing are buffer stops, the track to Stratford station being retained as a long siding. The original Stratford upon Avon temporary terminus for the Honeybourne branch was at Sanctuary Lane, (now known as Sanctus Street) and this closed to passengers 1st January 1863 on the extension of the line to the new station (29.53 miles) in Alcester Road. Originally having a single platform on the 'Down' side, an 'Up' platform was added in 1891 and the 'Down' platform extended the following year. With the upgrading of the route, the curves at both ends of the station were eased from a radius of 18 chains to 25 chains, and a bay added at the 'Up' end of the 'Up' platform, this bay being converted into a loop 1st April 1911. The 'Down' main used Platform No.1, 550ft in length; the 'Up' main Platform No.2 measured 600ft, the south end of the 'Up' loop being No.3A and the northern end No.3B. The 'Up' loop reverted to an 'Up' bay 18th May 1969. The station closed to goods 6th May 1968.

The rather bleak Stratford upon Avon Race Course station, looking south, 19th April 1968.
(C.G. Maggs)

A Stephenson Locomotive Society special train at Stratford upon Avon, South Junction on 24th April 1965 with LMSR 4F 0-6-0 No. 44188.   *(W. Potter)*

The 4.15 p.m. Cardiff d.m.u. working at Stratford upon Avon station, 21st August 1958.
(R.E. Toop)

Locomotives

West Midland Railway 2-4-0 tank engine No.68 (GWR No.225) built by Beyer Peacock in 1861 worked the Honeybourne to Stratford branch. With the opening of the line from Honeybourne to Broadway, locomotives and coaches were used at first, though within a few weeks, the then novel steam railmotors were brought into operation. From 1908 when expresses were worked by 4-4-0s of the inside cylinder classes, generally of the 'Atbara' or 'Flower' classes, a representative of the 'County' class being used on the more prestigious Wolverhampton to Penzance trains, because Stonehouse Viaduct on the Midland line between Standish and Yate was not strong enough to support a 4-6-0, but in 1927 restrictions were reduced sufficiently to allow 'Saint' 4-6-0s over the line subject to a restriction of 30 mph over the viaduct. Since that date it was strengthened and 'Castles' permitted. The 4-4-0s were no mean performers over the line. 'Atbara' class 4-4-0 No.4142 *Brisbane* with 106 tons behind the tender is recorded as having sustained 56 mph up the 1 in 150 gradient from Bishop's Cleeve to Gotherington, reaching 80 mph on the descent to Honeybourne. Latterly the line's principal express, 'The Cornishman', was hauled either by a 'Castle' or a 'Hall' 4-6-0. Before dieselisation, Honeybourne to Stratford local services were covered by through Worcester and Evesham to Leamington or Birmingham workings handled by tender engines, 'Bulldogs' predominating until the early nineteen fifties when they were replaced by 2251 class 0-6-0s; 4300 2-6-0s; or more occasionally, BR Standard 2-6-0s.

Diesel traction first used the Cheltenham to Stratford line from 9th July 1934 when GWR railcars Nos. 2 to 4 with two 121 bhp engines capable of a maximum speed of 75-80 mph and having a seating capacity of 44 were introduced, a

'Castle' class 4-6-0 No. 7029 "Clun Castle" on the last steam hauled special from London, Paddington to Cheltenham Race Course, where depicted on 14th March 1963. (W. Potter)

GWR 'Atbara' class 4-4-0 No. 4140 nears Cheltenham Race Course station with a Taunton to Birmingham express on 30th July 1924. (H.G.W. Household)

'Star' class 4-6-0 No. 4061 "Glastonbury Abbey" passing Southam on 17th April 1952 with a Wolverhampton and Birmingham to Cheltenham Race Course train. (W. Potter)

ROD 2-8-0 No. 3006 heads a lengthy goods train at Bishop's Cleeve during wartime, November 1940. *(W. Potter)*

"Duke of Cornwall" class 4-4-0 No. 3289 on a 'Down' goods (two vans plus a brake van!) at Southam, May 1946. *(W. Potter)*

4300 class 2-6-0 No. 7304 on 25th July 1962 at Bishop's Cleeve on empty coaching stock. *(W. Potter)*

Several of the various GWR bogie diesel railcars worked the Honeybourne line over the years. Here W31 is seen at Malvern Road shed, Cheltenham on 30th October 1949.   *(W. Potter)*

supplement of 2s 6d (12½p) on the third class fare being charged. The railcars, equipped with a small buffet, worked express services from Birmingham to Cheltenham to Cardiff with stops only at Gloucester and Newport. A full service of two trains in each direction was inaugurated on 22nd September, but overcrowding due to the popularity of the service proved its undoing and steam haulage took over with its greater seating capacity. A hoped-for solution was the building in 1941 of railcars Nos.35—38 as two pairs of twin units capable of reaching a speed of 70 mph, with driving compartments at the extreme ends only, to replace the earlier single unit buffet cars. A standard coach could be coupled between the twin units to form a 3-car set. Cars Nos.36 and 38 had a buffet counter and Nos.35 and 37 lavatory accommodation. Despite a capacity of 168 passengers, the Birmingham to

GWR diesel railcar No. 25 with engine covers removed, stands outside Malvern Road shed, 14th March 1948—only a few weeks after nationalisation and still carrying its former owner's livery and coat of arms.   *(W. Potter)*

Water surges from the tank of 1400 class 0-4-2T No. 1424 as it departs from Hayles Abbey halt with auto coach W238, forming the 1.17 p.m. Honeybourne—Cheltenham train 27th February 1960.
(D.H. Ballantyne)

Cardiff train, once again diesel from November 1941, developed to such an extent that the diesel sets were soon only operating mid-week and they were eventually replaced by steam trains, made up to as many as 15 vehicles on occasions, the displaced diesel sets being deployed between Bristol and Weymouth and Reading and Newbury.

Freight was hauled by the various standard GWR goods locomotives and also during the Second World War by USA built Austerity 2-8-0s on loan to the GWR. Just before midnight on 17th November 1943, one such engine (No.2403) was working a freight train from Banbury to Margam via Leamington, Stratford upon Avon and Cheltenham. Instead of having plug cocks to the water gauge as generally used on British locomotives, it was fitted with a wheel-operated valve cock, which, if opened insufficiently, gave a false reading. This it did just before midnight, insufficient water causing the firebox crown to collapse and scald the fireman. In the blackout and confusion neither he nor his driver, realised how serious were his injuries and the brave man walked back nearly a mile to Honeybourne East Loop signal box to report the accident and ask for assistance. The signalman, an experienced ambulanceman, gave expert first aid, but the unfortunate fireman died of his injuries the following day.

The opening of Stratford Racecourse Junction in 1960 brought Eastern Region ex War Department and ex LMSR Stanier 2-8-0s (No.48402 being recorded) to join the 28xx 2-8-0s and BR Standard Class 9F 2-10-0s.

Collett 2884 class 2-8-0 No. 2891 heads a freight train near Gotherington on 25th July 1964.
(W. Potter)

Churchward 2800 class 2-8-0 No. 2801 on a 'Down' goods, as it passes under Southam road bridge on a sunny July day, 1945.
(W. Potter)

'Hall' class 4-6-0 No. 4949 "Packwood Hall" on a train of open wagons 16th July 1967 at Bishop's Cleeve.
(W. Potter)

Stanier 8F class 2-8-0 (ex-LMSR) No. 48109 with 'Up' iron ore empties, near Southam, 26th August 1964. *(W. Potter)*

Maximum Loading - Cheltenham Malvern Road to Stratford upon Avon, 1st October 1945:

'Castles' 455 tons.

'Stars', 'Halls', 'Granges', 'Saints', 31xx, 43xx, 56xx, 81xx, 420 tons.

3306—3455, 4400—4410, 36xx, 37xx, 45xx, 57xx, 77xx, 87xx, 97xx, 364 tons.

32xx, 2251, 0-6-2T 'B' Group 336 tons.

0-6-0, 0-6-0T, 0-6-2T 'A' Group 322 tons.

The last of the many — BR 9F class 2-10-0 No. 92220 "Evening Star" makes light work of a rake of iron ore empties near Cheltenham Race Course station on 4th May 1964, heading northwards. *(W. Potter)*

'Hall' class 4-6-0 No. 6926 "Holkham Hall" rounds the curve near Cheltenham Race Course with an iron ore train, 10th June 1964. *(W. Potter)*

On 17th June 1957 two of the four daily South Wales passenger trains were taken over by Inter City diesel multiple unit sets, on 10th March 1958 themselves being replaced by Cross-Country sets which also took over the remaining steam duties. Sunday services continued to have steam haulage for a couple of years which brought 'Britannia' Pacifics to the line. BR diesel sets and single car units took over the Stratford to Gloucester working, while freight was worked by diesel locomotives of classes 20, 31, 35, 37, 47 and 52.

BR Standard class 5, 4-6-0s were never a common sight on the line, but No. 73035 is seen here near Southam with a freight working, 18th June 1961. *(W. Potter)*

Summer excursion trains brought Britannia Pacifics to the line— No. 70053 minus its "Moray Firth" name-plates, pauses at Malvern Road station, 28th August 1965 on a Kingswear—Wolverhampton train. *(W. Potter)*

Class 47 Co Co diesel electric D1584 (later 47531) with a Sunday diversion from the Midland line, passing Cheltenham Race Course Station, 18th June 1967. *(W. Potter)*

LOCOMOTIVE SHEDS

Cheltenham

The timber-built shed measuring 161ft by 32ft at St. George's Road opened in October 1847. It had a gable-style slated roof with hipped ends and a large central louvre vent. It was necessarily closed in 1906, its site being required for Malvern Road Junction. It was replaced in 1907 by a new structure to the west of Malvern Road station. A standard two-road straight shed of brick construction, it measured 180ft by 38ft. The raised coal stage was a steel-framed structure with timber walls, the roof being a small water tank, a cantilevered awning from this tank sheltering coal wagons being unloaded. Two roads were added to the west side of the shed in April 1943 enlarging dimensions to 180ft by 66ft. The yard layout allowed for a 65ft turntable to be installed, but although tender engines were allocated, the feature was never constructed. It would have been rather a luxury because, if necessary, engines could be turned on the turntable at St. James' station or on the Hatherley Junction, Lansdown Junction, Gloucester Loop Junction triangle. The shed closed in October 1963 but the building remains intact to this day used by Sharpe & Fisher (Builders Merchants) Ltd who are fully aware of its history as there are a number of reminders of the past including the "GWR" letters which are carefully picked out on the iron entrance gates to the yard. Its GWR shed code was CHEL, but about 1936 when it became a sub shed to Gloucester, it was GLO, the code of the main shed. In the BR era it was a sub shed of 85B (Gloucester, Horton Road).

The brick built 2-road locomotive shed at Cheltenham, Malvern Road, 15th June 1933, as built in 1907.   *(P. Copeland)*

Malvern Road shed, as it was on 4th April 1958, with locomotives, left to right: 0-4-2T No. 1401; 2-6-2T No. 4139 and 0-6-0T No. 47422. *(W. Potter)*

Interior of Malvern Road shed with 'Prairie' tank locomotives Nos. 5518 and 4564 on the left. *(Collection L.B. Lapper)*

Malvern Road shed in June 1949 showing the 2-road extension of corrugated asbestos which was added in April 1943. Present are, left to right: 2-6-0 No. 6384; 0-6-0 No. 3213; and 2-6-2T's Nos. 5515 and 5574. (W. Potter)

No. 7815 "Fritwell Manor" poses outside the 1943 shed extension at Malvern Road, 2nd October 1949. (W. Potter)

GWR 0-4-2T No. 1401 at Malvern Road, 4th April 1958. On the left is Mogul No. 6330 and Prairie No. 4139, with 'Jinty' No. 47422 on the right. (W. Potter)

The raised coaling stage and water tank at Malvern Road depot, 15th June 1933.   (P. Copeland)

Locomotive allocation 31st December 1947:
4-6-0 No.7818 *Granville Manor.*
4-4-0 No.3449 *Nightingale.*
2-6-0s Nos.4320; 5345; 6326; 6341; 7303; 7312.
2-6-2Ts Nos.4141; 4534; 4564; 4567; 4578; 5515; 5538; 5574.
0-4-2T No.1402.
Diesel railcar No.25.

'Bulldog' class 4-4-0 No. 3447 "Jackdaw" comes off-shed at Malvern Road, September 1944.
(W. Potter)

Honeybourne

This single road shed built near the 'Down' end of the 'Up' platform in 1853 was demolished in 1907 in order to enlarge the yard. Its replacement built in 1909 was burnt down two years later on 13th September 1911 and was not reconstructed, only a small covered coaling platform being provided. The first shed measured 65ft by 20ft and the second 66ft by 15ft, the latter having brick walls and a slated gable-style roof. Its principal occupant was the Honeybourne shunting engine. As Honeybourne was a sub shed of Worcester, engines allocated to Honeybourne were given the GWR code WOS or the BR code 85A. In 1954, of the two Collett 0-6-0s stabled there, one was used for shunting in the yard and the other for assisting goods trains up Camden Bank. The depot closed in December 1965. Although a 40ft turntable was installed when the Stratford branch opened, it was removed many years ago, not being shown on an 1890 map.

Allocation January 1901:
0-6-0STs Nos.650; 1775.

Stratford upon Avon

The single road OWWR shed immediately south of the overbridge south of the station, opened 1st January 1863 replacing a temporary shed at Sanctuary Lane which had a 40ft turntable. Measuring 59ft 6ins by 14ft 7ins, it had timber walls constructed on low brick walls, the slated roof having gables. The shed closed in October 1910 being replaced by a larger two-road shed, 155ft by 38ft, at the opposite end of the station, both the shed and coaling stage being similar to those at Cheltenham, and like Cheltenham, there was no turntable. A sub shed to Tyseley, engines bore the GWR code TYS, or BR code 84E. Stratford shed closed 10th September 1962.

Allocation 1st January 1901: 0-4-2T No.1431.
31st December 1947: 0-6-0s Nos. 2206; 2297. 2-6-2Ts Nos. 3151; 3180.

Train Services—Local

The train service from Honeybourne to Stratford began with five 'Down' and four 'Up' daily and one each way on Sundays, though by 1860, four trains ran on weekdays and two on Sundays, with three each way on Sundays in July and August. Through trains began running between Worcester and Leamington via Stratford from August 1861. The train service for August 1887 showed four trains daily from Leamington, through Stratford to Honeybourne and five in the reverse direction with no Sunday service south of Stratford. By 1902 this service had increased to six and seven respectively while in 1938 nine 'Down' and ten 'Up' trains ran daily, with three on Sundays. With the closure of the two intermediate stations on 3rd January 1966, services from Honeybourne to Stratford were reduced to morning and evening.

2-6-2T No. 5161 departs from Stratford upon Avon with a southbound train 6th April 1953. No. 5164 waits at the next platform, this loco is now preserved on the Severn Valley Railway.
(L.B. Lapper)

In April 1910 seven railmotors ran each way between Honeybourne and Cheltenham, some to and from Evesham, one additional service being run from Honeybourne to Broadway and back. In July 1932, six one-class only railmotors ran from Honeybourne to Cheltenham and return, plus three each way between Cheltenham and Broadway, one Cheltenham to Toddington and back and one Honeybourne to Winchcombe and return. Two ran each way Honeybourne to Cheltenham on Sundays. The local passenger service was withdrawn on 7th March 1960.

Steam railmotor No. 40 at Toddington on a Cheltenham—Honeybourne local service, 28th July 1910.
(H.G.W. Household)

A Winchcombe-Cheltenham auto train, near Cheltenham Race Course station with 0-4-2T No. 562 in charge, 24th July 1924.   (H.G.W. Household)

A 2-car auto train leaves Bishop's Cleeve, headed by 0-4-2T No.4841 on a May evening 1946.
(W. Potter)

No. 5538, a 2-6-2T pulls out from Bishop's Cleeve in July 1941 with a Honeybourne-Cheltenham, St. James' train. *(W. Potter)*

Train Services—Through

The first through train over part of the line was a regular excursion in 1907 on Mondays and Saturdays from Wolverhampton to Winchcombe via Stratford. From 1st July 1908, (the date of opening of the North Warwickshire line which gave direct access to Birmingham), a through train service was run from Wolverhampton and Birmingham, via, Stratford and Cheltenham to the West of England, providing the first regular through service between Birmingham and Cornwall. As a result of a High Court Injunction obtained by the Midland Railway, it had to follow that Company's route between Yate and Bristol. The MR never disputed the GWR's right to run over Midland metals from Standish Junction, but it intended that once on the line, Great Western trains must continue and not leave at Yate where the GWR had its own independent route to Bristol Temple Meads. This amazing contention was actually upheld by the first court before which the case was tried, but R.R. Nelson, solicitor to the GWR, insisted on appealing and when the matter came before the House of Lords—the third court to hear the case—the Great Western won without even its counsel being called. To avoid reversal into or out of the GWR station at Gloucester, the GWR planned to build a new station at Chequers Road Junction, (later renamed Gloucester South), but the plan was abandoned because so many difficulties arose with the Gloucester City Corporation regarding approaches. The result was that trains from Stratford omitted Gloucester until 1952 when the former LMSR station at Eastgate was used.

Also in 1908, a morning train ran from Cardiff to Leamington, Rugby, Peterborough and the Great Eastern Railway to Norwich, but lacking popularity, it was soon withdrawn. By April 1910 there were three expresses daily between

Stratford and Cheltenham: the Wolverhampton to Penzance which covered the 29¾ miles in 31 minutes; the Wolverhampton to Weston super Mare which took 34 minutes; while the 'Shakespeare Express' from Birkenhead to Bristol took 33 minutes for this line. In the 'Up' direction, the Weston super Mare train started from Torquay. In 1914 the train from Birkenhead carried a through coach to Cardiff. All long distance services were suspended for a time during the latter part of the First World War and it was not until the nineteen-twenties that the through passenger traffic really developed with increasing services to South Wales as well as the West of England. It was during this period that at times on summer Saturdays, traffic was so heavy that the Wolverhampton to Penzance express had to be run in no less than four parts. In July 1932 three trains ran from Wolverhampton to the West of England; one Wolverhampton to Carmarthen (on Saturdays-only it conveyed coaches from Birmingham to Weymouth); and one Birmingham to Weston super Mare. In the reverse direction, three ran from the West of England to Wolverhampton; one from South Wales to Birmingham and one from Taunton to Birmingham. Extra trains on summer Saturdays ran from Birmingham to the West of England; two from Birmingham to Weston super Mare; one Wolverhampton to Ilfracombe and in the reverse direction: one Taunton to Birmingham; Highbridge to Birmingham; the West of England to Birmingham; two Paignton to Wolverhampton; Weston super Mare to Wolverhampton and Weymouth to Birmingham.

In July 1938 through coaches ran from Wolverhampton to Weston super Mare and Paignton; a buffet railcar from Birmingham to Cardiff, (non-stop Birmingham to Cheltenham); followed by a steam-hauled train from Birmingham to South Wales; Wolverhampton to Penzance except Saturdays when its destinations were Minehead and Ilfracombe. Extra trains on summer Saturdays ran from Birmingham to Paignton; Wolverhampton to Penzance; two trains from Birmingham to Weston super Mare and Wolverhampton to Paignton. On Sundays a train ran from Wolverhampton to Penzance. In the 'Up' direction there was the Cardiff to Birmingham railcar; the Penzance to Wolverhampton; Cardiff to Birmingham, (Pembroke Dock and Tenby to Birmingham on Saturdays); Paignton to Birmingham; Taunton to Birmingham; with extra trains on summer Saturdays Highbridge and Weston super Mare to Birmingham; two Weston super Mare to Birmingham and one Paignton to Birmingham. The Second World War caused the suspension of through trains from 25th September 1939 to 1st October 1945.

On 30th June 1952 the Wolverhampton to Penzance service received the title 'The Cornishman'. Unlike its unnamed predecessors, at Gloucester it diverged to Eastgate station. Taunton was served by a slip coach. Through coaches, detached and attached at Exeter were run between Wolverhampton and Kingswear. From 10th September 1962 'The Cornishman' and the South Wales dmus were diverted via Birmingham New Street and Ashchurch, 'The Cornishman' saving 38 minutes between Birmingham and Bristol, but summer-only locomotive hauled trains

A Torquay—Wolverhampton express with through carriages for Plymouth, near Cheltenham Race Course on 24th July 1924. Motive power is provided by 4-4-0 No. 3816 "County of Leicester".
(H.G.W. Household)

continued to run over the Honeybourne route on Friday nights and Saturdays until 1966. From the same date, two connecting services with the South Wales trains ran between Leamington Spa, Stratford, Cheltenham and Gloucester provided initially by 3-car dmus, but as they were lightly patronised, by late 1964 were replaced by a single one-class unit. These were the last regular passenger trains over the Honeybourne line, and ceased from 23rd March 1968. The Cheltenham stop had been omitted from 3rd January 1966 as Malvern Road and St. James' both closed to passenger traffic on that date. Summer Saturday services to the south west calling at Stratford continued to be routed over the line until 1966 when there were four such trains.

From 1st July 1907 the 4.45 pm Paddington to Wolverhampton slipped a coach for Cheltenham and Moreton in Marsh, regular stops being made at Broadway and Winchcombe, though passengers from London could be set down at Weston sub Edge, Toddington, Gotherington or Bishop's Cleeve on informing the guard at Moreton in Marsh, Cheltenham passengers arriving 2 hours 50 minutes after leaving Paddington, this train providing the fastest late afternoon service from Paddington to Cheltenham. With the exception of special race trains, this was the only long distance service which ever called at intermediate stations on the line, apart from a short-lived fast diesel railcar service introduced in the early nineteen-fifties between Gloucester and Birmingham Snow Hill which called at Broadway in each direction. The 4.45 pm from Paddington also carried a slip coach for Stratford which set down at Long Marston and Milcote on notice being given to the guard at

Moreton in Marsh. The coaches proceeded from Moreton in Marsh via South Loop Junction to the East Loop Junction where the first portion continued to Stratford and the rear to Cheltenham. From 22nd March 1915 the working ceased, it being the final regular passenger use of the South Loop Junction to East Loop Junction, though it was used by diverted trains and excursions from the Eastern Region via Bletchley and Yarnton. Regular freight traffic ceased from 1st March 1965 and the line closed 13th October the same year. In July 1907 two regular excursions used the curve; one on Thursdays from Paddington to Stratford and one on Mondays and Saturdays from Wolverhampton to Winchcombe.

Gloucester R.C.&W. built single car diesel unit M55002 draws out from Malvern Road station, 24th July 1965 on a Gloucester—Leamington Spa run.   *(W. Potter)*

A Wolverhampton—Taunton through train, 25th July 1964 headed by 'Castle' class 4-6-0 No. 5063 "Earl Baldwin", near Gotherington. *(W. Potter)*

A train from the south coast for Birmingham Snow Hill and Wolverhampton passing Bishop's Cleeve, 4th September 1965 with the power of 'Britannia' 4-6-2 No. 70053 (formerly "Moray Firth") to the fore. *(W. Potter)*

6803 "Bucklebury Grange" passes Southam in the snow on 11th March 1965 with a Gold Cup race special from Wolverhampton Low Level to Cheltenham Race Course station. (W. Potter)

'Hymek' B-B diesel hydraulic D7095 leaving Cheltenham Race Course station, 7th March 1964 with empty stock. This train had been worked through from Carmarthen. (W. Potter)

Motor Trolley System of Maintenance

The line from Stratford to Honeybourne was maintained by the motor trolley system. Petrol driven trolleys built by D. Wickham of Ware, Herts were 15ft in length with accommodation for 16 men in addition to materials and equipment and were capable of being driven from either end. A trolley stabled on the 'Up' refuge siding spur at Stratford worked from there each day, returning in the evening, this being more economical than having shorter sections looked after by gangers. Time allowances of the trolley for the guidance of signalmen were:

	Mins
Stratford upon Avon	—
Milcote	6½
Long Marston	5
Honeybourne North	6

The trolley was limited to an upper speed limit of 40 mph.

A permanent way train, hauled by 0-6-2T No. 5677 passes through Hayles Abbey halt in the 'Down' direction in 1960.   (P.J. Garland)

The exterior of Cheltenham St. James station, photographed 25th August 1951.   (L.B. Lapper)

The Branch to Cheltenham St. James' Station

Following the 1844 Act for the amalgamation of the Cheltenham & Great Western Union Railway with the GWR, a branch was built from the main Birmingham to Gloucester line to provide a more convenient station closer to the town centre than that at Lansdown Road. Cheltenham Spa (St. James'), 43 chains from Malvern Road, opened on 23rd October 1847 as Cheltenham; was renamed Cheltenham St. James' on 11th May 1908, finally becoming Cheltenham Spa (St. James') on 1st February 1925.

Originally it had two platform roads and two central carriage sidings, but was reconstructed in the early years of this century. An imposing, brick-built terminal station with a covered carriage approach fronting St. James' Square, it had two curved semi-island platforms and two central carriage sidings. Signalling was arranged so that arrivals used the two northern platforms, (in 1956 these platforms were lengthened by 150ft), but trains could depart from any road.

The station dealt with traffic to and from Gloucester and London, Kingham and Honeybourne. It was the starting point of the prestigious 'Cheltenham Flyer' introduced on 9th July 1923, and which was to become the world's fastest steam train. Progress from Cheltenham to Swindon was nothing out of the ordinary, the speed section being between Swindon and Paddington. Its fastest recorded journey was made on 6th June 1932 when the 77.3 miles between these points were covered in 56 minutes 47 seconds, producing an average speed of 81.7 mph.

From 3rd November 1958 St. James' was served by trains from the former Midland & South Western Junction line from Southampton, until their withdrawal

A general view of St. James' station in 1965 with the goods shed visible on the right, with a class 08 0-6-0 diesel shunter alongside and a d.m.u. in the station. (L.B. Lapper)

A panoramic view of St. James' on 6th August 1965 with 2-6-2T No. 4100 on an evening goods ready for departure to Gloucester. (W. Potter)

7029 "Clun Castle" on an evening goods train for Gloucester, about to depart from Cheltenham St. James' goods yard. (W. Potter)

"Dukedog" 4-4-0 No. 9017 after arrival at St. James' station, 20th April 1958. This locomotive survives and is now on the Bluebell Railway, Sussex where it re-entered service in mid 1982 following a complete overhaul.   *(W. Potter)*

4300 class 2-6-0 No. 5305 is turned on the turntable at St. James', 10th September 1961. This was the occasion of the Railway Correspondence & Travel Society special last train over the Midland & South Western Junction Railway.   *(L.B. Lapper)*

The last steam working from Cheltenham St. James' station on 12th June 1965. This was operated for Charlton Kings Sunday School, being an excursion to Weston-super-Mare and was worked by 7029 "Clun Castle". *(W. Potter)*

on 9th September 1961; the end of the Kingham service came on 15th October 1962. The number of trains using the station was then insufficient to make it an economic proposition to retain and since through Birmingham to Gloucester trains using the former Midland Railway route could not use it, this convenient central station was closed and all trains used Lansdown St. James' was closed to passengers on 3rd January 1966 and to goods on 31st October the same year. The goods yard accommodated 475 wagons and the goods shed, 205ft in length, sited to the north of the passenger station, contained four, 1½ ton cranes.

The end of the line?—or it could have been. . .the last BR train on the Honeybourne Line, a permanent way working at 17.00 hrs on 14th August 1977 heading northwards, about to pass under the Worcester—Oxford line. This was hauled by class 25 Bo Bo diesel electric No. 25 325.

(Simon James)

Foreigner at Malvern Road 1. LNER J25 class 0-6-0 No. 2076 on loan to the GWR during World War II. Photographed shunting goods wagons 11th April 1940. (L.B. Lapper)

Foreigner at Malvern Road 2. Bo Bo diesel railcar No. B23 en route for delivery to Central Argentina, 5th September 1937. (L.B. Lapper)

Preservation — the New GWR

Following the announcement by British Railways that it proposed to close the line, the Gloucestershire Warwickshire Railway Society was formed at a public meeting held at Willersey village hall on 18th August 1976. Initially, the aim was to persuade BR that there were very good reasons for the retention and operation of the line. Failing this, the Society would attempt to acquire and run the line as a private, tourist railway. Local response was most encouraging with membership soon approaching the 1,000 mark including area groups formed at Cheltenham, Evesham and Stratford.

Formal closure of the line, excepting Honeybourne—Long Marston, took effect from 1st November 1976 and the Society deposited a sum of £1,000 with the British Railways Property Board so that purchase negotiations could take place. However, at the end of the year BR reversed its decision regarding disposal and stated the line would remain under operational control. The junction at Cheltenham (Lansdown) was removed in November and all the fishplate bolts were loosened, whilst various maintenance work was undertaken from time to time. This

Inset: The scene at Toddington, 24th January 1981, looking north from the signal box. The track had been lifted but the ballast remained in situ. (P.D. Nicholson)

The same spot, six months later, 20th June 1981, only three months after the Gloucestershire Warwickshire Railway had taken up a lease of the site. A gang lay track alongside the goods shed to accommodate incoming stock, whilst 2-8-0 No. 2807 is prepared for off-loading onto the centre road, and on the right the Hudswell Clarke diesel is started up. (P.D. Nicholson)

situation remained until July 1979 when track lifting by contractors commenced. Track materials were collected up and transported by road vehicles, the work starting at Winchcombe where track panels were stacked, and dismantled before removal from site.

British Railways still maintained that the line was not for sale, saying it was to be retained as a "contingency" for the future. Then, in August 1980 a letter was sent by Sir Peter Parker, then Chairman of the British Railways Board to Michael Spicer MP and Charles Irving MP informing them that due to the financial position facing the Board it was now considered sensible to release the land, from Cheltenham to Honeybourne and Long Marston to Stratford upon Avon. The Honeybourne-Long Marston section has been retained for use by BR.

The Society immediately began discussions with all relevant organisations as well as investigating various methods of raising finance. By this time membership of the G.W.R.S. had, not surprisingly fallen and was then standing at about 400. By January 1981 the Society had reached agreement in principle with the British Railways Property Board to purchase the whole of the railway trackbed, Cheltenham (Pittville) to Honeybourne and Long Marston to Stratford upon Avon (Regional boundary), a total distance of approximately 22 miles, for £25,000. The overall condition of the structures on the line was considered good, having been built to a high standard and the ballast was still in situ with any remaining buildings and signalling equipment being included. The value of the land was calculated by BR on the basis that the Company would be taking on the responsibility of the liability of bridges, tunnels, embankments etc. These items have in effect, negative value, which is off set against the positive value of the more useful areas of land, such as the goods yards. Hence the overall cost of acquisition was at a considerably reduced figure.

The Society instructed Parliamentary Agents to apply for the grant of a Light Railway Order to ensure that the sale of the line would not be subsequently delayed and ensure that passenger carrying operations could be commenced as soon as possible.

As the first step towards eventual operation a lease was taken out on Toddington yard from 24th March 1981, with the first working party attending the site on 28th March. Following initial site clearance work a few lengths of track were laid in anticipation of the arrival of locomotives and rolling stock. A security compound was built alongside the old goods shed, which at that time was leased to an industrial concern. The signal box was also included within the compound although it was rather a case of shutting the stable door. . .the Gwili Railway Preservation Society having removed the lever frame etc only a matter of days before, which they had purchased, just as the G.W.R.S. finalised their negotiations with another department of BR.

The first locomotive to arrive at Toddington was Hudswell Clarke D615, an 0-6-0 diesel of 1938 which was delivered on 30th May. This was followed by the

Toddington signal box—before. Photographed 24th January 1981 having suffered at the hands of vandals. (P.D. Nicholson)

Toddington signal box—after. Photographed May 1982 during restoration by the GWR S. & T. Department. A lever frame, the windows and steps have all now been reinstated and it is a good indication as to the thoroughness of restoration being undertaken by this preserved railway. (P.D. Nicholson)

Hudswell Clarke D615, a vintage 0-6-0 diesel of 1938, propels No. 5952 "Cogan Hall" at Toddington on a February evening 1982. (P.D. Nicholson)

Churchward designed GWR 2800 class 2-8-0 No. 2807 was the first steam locomotive to arrive for the 'new GWR'. This engine, owned by Cotswold Steam Preservation Ltd. is currently being restored to full working order. Seen here at Toddington on arrival, 20th June 1981.

(P.D. Nicholson)

first steam locomotive on 20th June, ex GWR Churchward 2800 class 2-8-0 No.2807 purchased by Cotswold Steam Preservation Ltd from Woodham Bros, Barry. This arrived late on a Saturday afternoon in fine weather, the spectacle attracting a huge crowd. Low-loading lorries continued to arrive from Barry for the rest of that week, bringing 'Manor' class 4-6-0 7821 *Ditcheat Manor* on the 23rd, three 3,500 gallon tenders on the 25th and 7828 *"Odney Manor"* on the 27th. The two 'Manors' are owned by the Great Western Steam Locomotives Group whose third engine from Barry, 'Hall' class 4-6-0 5952 *"Cogan Hall"'* arrived at Toddington on 16th September 1981. The weekend of 11th and 12th July witnessed the arrival of two former National Coal Board steam locomotives, *"King George"*, Hunslet 2409 of 1942, 0-6-0 saddle tank and Peckett 1976 of 1939, 0-4-0 saddle tank. Both are privately owned and are undergoing restoration to working order.

The boiler and firebox is lifted from 7821 Ditcheat Manor at Toddington, 19.8.81 in preparation for restoration. *(P.D. Nicholson)*

A considerable amount of rolling stock was soon acquired, both by the Company and privately, with items being purchased direct from BR, industrial concerns and even other preserved railways and centres. The first item of coaching stock to arrive was a particularly interesting and appropriate vehicle, GWR Auto trailer No.169. This had survived in remarkably original condition in use as an office at the nearby Horton Road Diesel Depot, Gloucester. Later the same day, 19th August 1981, two more ex GWR coaches were delivered to Toddington, these coming from Worcester where they had been part of a breakdown train.

All this activity created a high degree of interest locally at least, with extensive media coverage which resulted in an increase in society membership once again. It was decided that a public company would need to be formed for the purpose of acquiring and operating such a line. The company was registered on 28th July 1981 as 'The Gloucestershire Warwickshire Steam Railway Public Limited Company' with the share prospectus being issued on 8th August. The share issue opened at 10.00am on 20th August with 400,000 ordinary shares at £1 each at par with a minimum application of 20.

The minimum legal requirement was set at £50,000 to be raised by 16th September 1981. This was easily achieved, with £73,310 being subscribed within the statutory 40 days. The sale of shares continues of course and is now well past the 100,000 mark. After payment of the formation expenses, the Company was able to purchase a large quantity of track materials, a water tower and a turntable from BR at Ashford, Kent, four ex GWR coaches converted for use as camping vehicles at Dawlish Warren, Devon, various items of plant and machinery — and a complete narrow gauge railway.

The major site work to date has been concentrated at Toddington where the transformation of the station and yard area during the first four years of occupation must go down as one of the most remarkable achievements in railway preservation history. Extensive sidings have been laid to accommodate the now huge collection of locomotives and rolling stock, as well as double track through the station and on towards the viaduct north of the station. The station building has been thoroughly refurbished, the platform reinstated, the signal box fully restored — complete with a replacement lever frame from Earlswood Lakes, near Birmingham and the goods shed established as a workshop and office.

The body of GWR Auto coach No. 169 is gently lowered back on to its bogies at Toddington following transport by road from Gloucester on 19th August 1981.   *(P.D. Nicholson)*

With so much intense activity and so many go-ahead people involved, almost inevitably 'political' problems occurred on the way. However, this appears to have been largely overcome by the formation of a new supporters organisation in mid 1982. Initially known as the Cheltenham & Stratford Railway Association it subsequently became the Cheltenham & Stratford Railway Limited, a company limited by guarantee, on 1st May 1983. The stated aims are to give financial support to the PLC, promote the growth of area support groups, provide off-site sales and publicity, to work in close co-operation with the Railway's own departments, keep members informed and to encourage as many as possible to take an active role in securing the future of the line. More recently it has been agreed that the CSR should take full operational responsibility for the railway, under the financial control of the PLC.

The CSR also runs the very successful 'Rapid Extension Fund' which is designed to encourage a large number of regular monthly contributors which provides finance exclusively for use to extend the railway, first to Winchcombe, then to Broadway. This covers the cost of track materials and maintenance of the formation. All contributions received that are sufficient to make up a block are converted into shares in the PLC every March. Any small balances are carried forward and included in the next share issue. The scheme has proved to be very worthwhile and has enabled the railway to purchase several large quantities of track materials.

The exterior of Toddington station, 31st January 1985. Restoration of this original GWR building from near dereliction is now well advanced. (P.D. Nicholson)

The weekend 29-30th August 1981 saw a 24 hour sponsored track laying session by members of the G.W.R.S. resulting in 269 yards of track being laid and about £600 in cash raised. The night shift lower a rail into position during the early hours of the 30th.   *(P.D. Nicholson)*

The narrow gauge railway previously referred to, has been an interesting and unusual development in view of the scope of the main project and one which was not originally envisaged. Several members with an interest in such railways realised that an ideal setting for a 2ft gauge line existed along the western boundary of Toddington yard. The edge of the yard was at a slightly lower level than the main area, making what appeared to be a small cutting. This formed a potential trackbed for an attractive line, as well as being unobtrusive for most of its length, so would not detract from the authenticity of the main project.

Local narrow gauge enthusiast, Bob Washington was approached as he had, at that time, a well equipped 2ft gauge line at his Cheltenham home. It was not long before various items began to arrive at Toddington and an initial start made on what was known as the Cotswold Narrow Gauge Railway. A narrow gauge group of working members was formed to clear the 'trackbed', and to lay track using 25-40lb/yd rail on ½ BR wooden sleepers and ballast transferred from the main trackbed. There were various legalities going through at the time which somewhat restricted on-site activities with regard to the standard gauge, so this did not inhibit any work in that direction, and in fact gave several members something to do in the meantime.

81

2ft gauge 'Tiny Tim' 0-4-0 diesel, Hunslet 5222 attempts to plough its way through the snow in December 1981, in conditions that resulted in the cancellation of the appearance of Santa Claus!
(R.J. Washington)

Motor Rail 26007, a 10HP, 4-wheel diesel on the 2ft gauge Cotswold Narrow Gauge Railway at Toddington, 14th July 1982, with the 4-wheel passenger coach.
(P.D. Nicholson)

It was also realised that such a line could be made operational far quicker than the main line so giving visitors something to see, and at the same time bring in some additional revenue. Construction began in September 1981 and this was sufficiently advanced by the end of the year to advertise 'Santa Specials' for the weekend 12-13th December, for which a large quantity of mince pies was ordered. However, the extreme weather conditions of that week resulted in a last minute cancellation as the site became virtually inaccessible due to deep snow drifts, to such an extent that it was thought even Santa could not get through. At some places the narrow gauge cutting was completely filled with snow! (It is understood that several members lived on an almost exclusive diet of mince pies well into 1982).

The NG line was formally inspected by Mr. L. Abbott of the Railway Inspectorate on 20th May 1982 and passed for operation, subject to a few small items requiring attention, the most major of which was the erection of fencing along the operating length of the line. Public services commenced on 29th May using Motor Rail 26007, a 10HP 4-wheel diesel and a 4-wheel passenger coach acquired from the Cheadle Moseley Industrial Tramway Museum at Stockport, Greater Manchester. The track was about 200 yards in length and apart perhaps, for a slight extension, and the addition of a further locomotive or two, this could well have been the limit of narrow gauge activities at Toddington.

Towards the end of 1982, amid a certain amount of secrecy, negotiations took place between members of the GWR and the Dowty Railway Preservation Society. This long established organisation was based at Ashchurch, near Tewkesbury, about ten miles away. The landlords, Dowty Mining Equipment Ltd required the site for industrial development and had asked the railway society to find alternative accommodation. Dowty offered to assist with financing the move together with covered accommodation at a new site.

Agreement was reached for the transfer of the entire stock to Toddington, which in fact was a very beneficial move for both organisations involved. The DRPS has a large collection of standard gauge equipment, including a working steam locomotive, *Cadbury*, an Avonside 0-4-0T and a couple of Great Western coaches. Also, they had a very extensive and well equipped 2ft gauge railway at Ashchurch which was operated on occasional open days each season.

The move of equipment began in January 1983 and was completed on 15th July with the arrival of the two coaches. The shed at Ashchurch was moved and now houses the SG stock whilst a new shed was erected for the NG line, which has been greatly extended and improved. This is now operated under the full control of the Dowty R.P.S. (which was re-titled the North Gloucestershire Railway Society, during 1985) using steam power regularly. From being little more than a 'side show' the narrow gauge is now an important and popular aspect of railway operations at Toddington.

Formal application for the Light Railway order for the Gloucestershire Warwickshire Railway was made at the end of November 1982, followed by a period in which any objections could be made. In the event this brought forth five — the County Councils of Gloucestershire and Hereford & Worcester, the Severn Trent Water Authority, the Gas Council and a private householder in Cheltenham.

Agreements were reached with all parties by October 1983 and details were submitted to the Department of Transport for their further consideration. The result was the granting of the LRO on 24th December 1983, without need for a public enquiry and compared with many such applications this was very speedily obtained indeed.

This enabled the purchase of the first section of the line to proceed and this was completed on 24th February 1984. The British Railways Property Board agreed to the sale of the section from the Cheltenham Borough Boundary at Pittville to the first overline bridge north of Broadway, a distance of 14½ miles for a figure of £15,000. Included in this are three railway yards at Winchcombe, Toddington and Broadway, the fully ballasted trackbed, 30 miles of fencing, 28 rail overbridges, 12 rail underbridges, 36 culverts, two tunnels and a viaduct.

Official inspection of the site at Toddington was made by Major Rose of the Railway Inspectorate on 21st March 1984 with initial clearance being given for the operation of a 2-coach push and pull train over a ¼ mile section. Formal re-opening soon took place after this when the tape was cut at Toddington station on Easter Sunday, 22nd April 1984 by local M.P., the Secretary of State for Transport, Mr. Nicholas Ridley.

"Justine", Jung No.939 of 1906, an 0-4-0 well tank, heads a two-coach train on the N.G. line, 22.4.84, the first day of steam operations. This locomotive was acquired from Belgium in 1974 by members of Dowty R.P.S.

(P.D. Nicholson)

Ex BR No. D9537, still carrying its former owners number '52', outside the goods shed at Toddington on 19th March 1983. Note the new doors that have been fitted to the end of the shed, this end having previously been bricked up. In the background another class 14 0-6-0 diesel hydraulic '51' (BR No. D9539) awaits attention. (P.D. Nicholson)

Rebuilt Bulleid Pacific No. 35006 'Peninsular & Oriental S.N. Co.' at Toddington on 26th March 1983, a week after its arrival from Barry. Owned by the 35006 Association it is now being restored to working order, and when completed will be fitted with a brand new tender specially built for it. (P.D. Nicholson)

Opening Day — 22nd April 1984.
'Cadbury' (Avonside No. 1977, 0-4-0T) in smart red livery works out from Toddington station on the first day of passenger services. For such an important occasion the locomotive's headboard was a somewhat inappropriate appendage, reading as it did — "22nd Year Dowty Railway Society"!
(P.D. Nicholson)

The coach used for the first season of operations was ex BR Mk. 1 corridor second, speedily adapted for push-pull working. Livery was chocolate and cream but its BR number, E25020 was not carried.
(P.D. Nicholson)

Toddington station, 31st January 1985, looking north. Compare this with the view in the same direction four years earlier on page 74. (P.D. Nicholson)

Trains were worked for the first season by ex BR class 14 0-6-0 diesel hydraulic No.D9537 owned by the Cotswold Diesel Preservation Group and *Cadbury*, Avonside No.1977, 0-4-0 side tank, owned by Dowty R.P.S. BR Mk I coach, E25020, a corridor second has been adapted for push-pull operation and painted in chocolate and cream livery. The first three weekends of train operations witnessed in excess of 4,000 visitors to the site.

Services in 1984 ran as far as Didbrook Bridge (¼ mile), but the terminus for 1985 will be Hayles Abbey Halt (1 mile), the track being laid to there in June 1984. Track should have been extended right through to Winchcombe (2½ miles) by the end of 1985 ready for re-opening in 1986.

Unlike Toddington there is neither a station building nor a signal box at Winchcombe, so along with all the other facilities required these too will have to be reinstated. A signal box has been acquired from Hall Green, Birmingham, this now having been dismantled and transported ready for re-erection on the foundations of the original structure. The station building presents an even greater task and for this the old GWR Monmouth Troy building is being obtained. This will have to be dismantled stone by stone and re-assembled at Winchcombe.

This then, is the story of the 'Honeybourne Line', so far. Under its second lease of life it has become one of Britain's most ambitious railway preservation projects. The enthusiasm and dedication already demonstrated over the first four years at Toddington clearly shows that one day perhaps it will be possible to see a double track, GWR steam hauled main line railway in operation once again — despite all the odds. . .

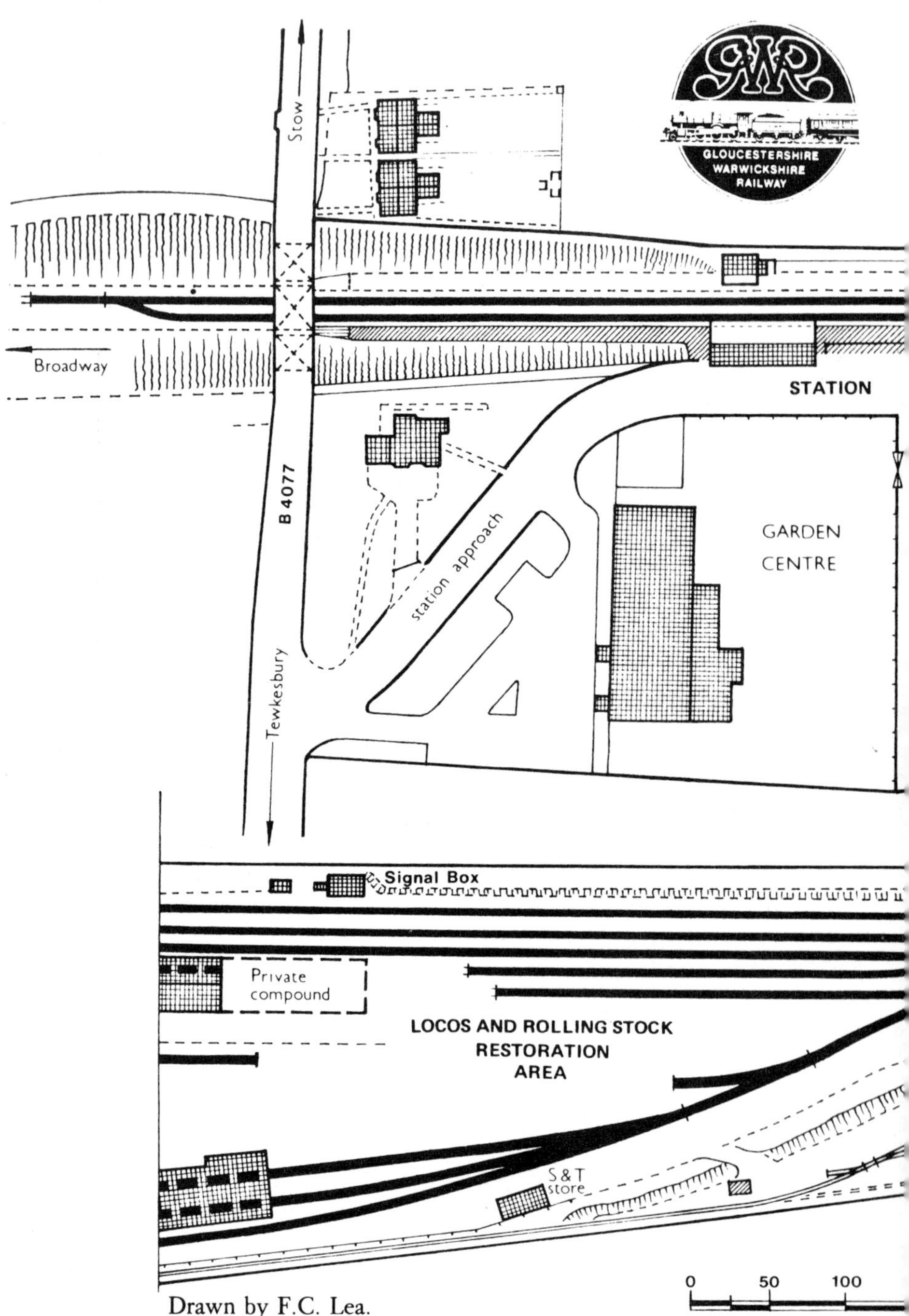

Drawn by F.C. Lea.

Gloucestershire Warwickshire Railway
TODDINGTON
LAYOUT PLAN

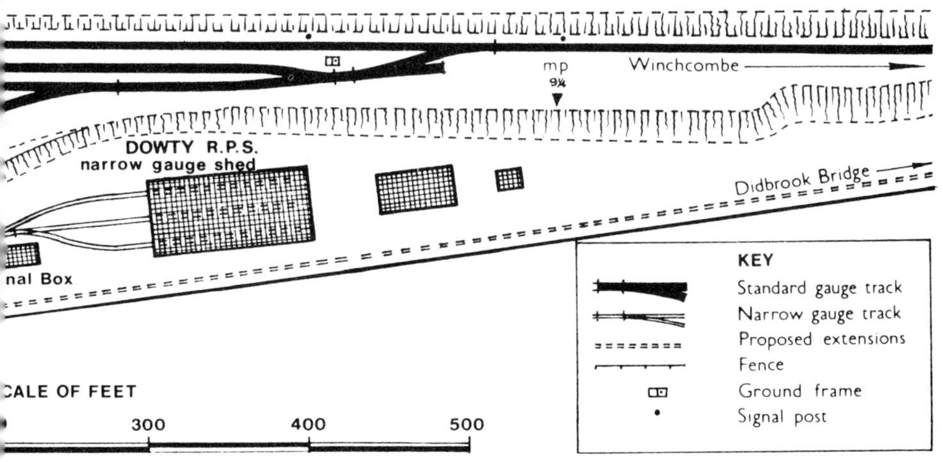

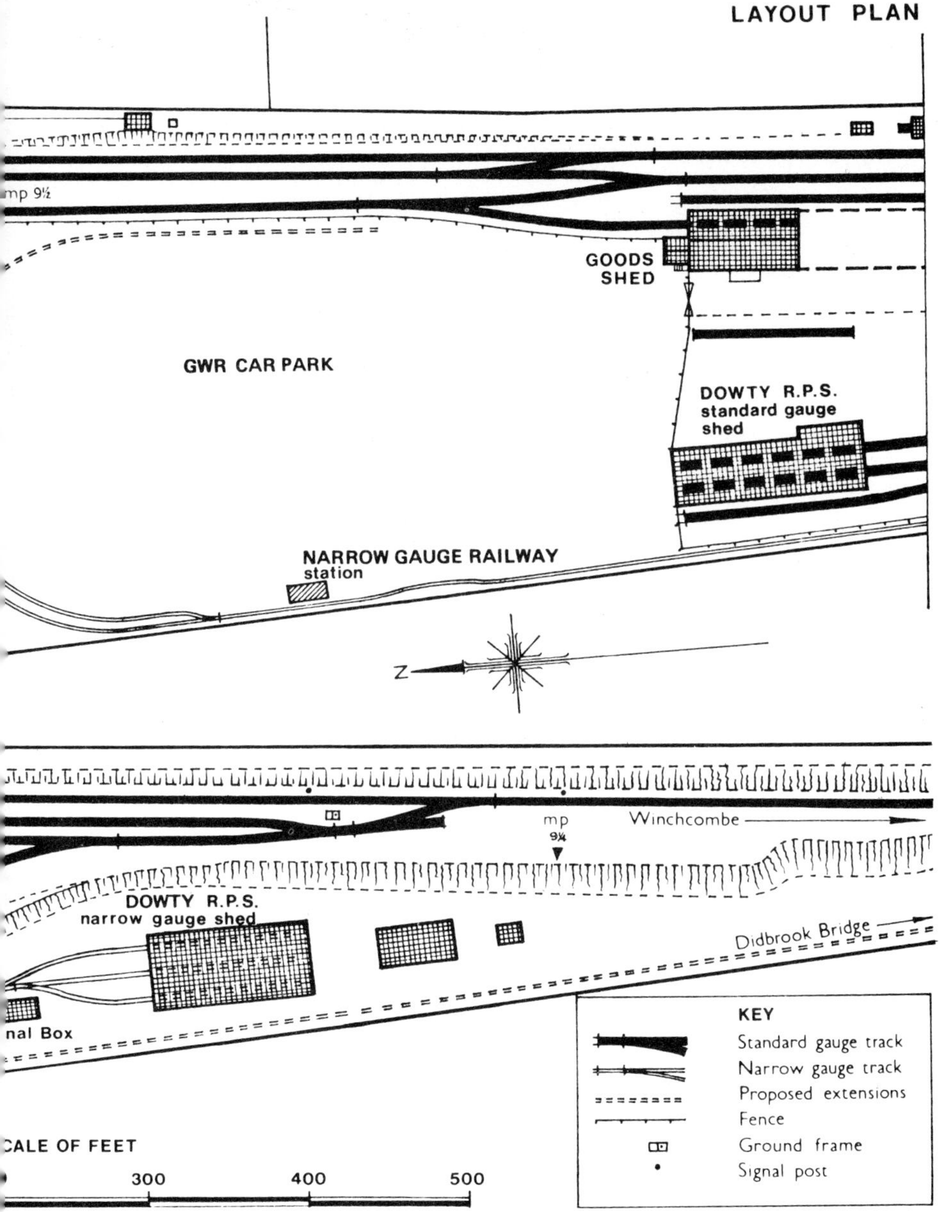

GWR Station Track Diagrams

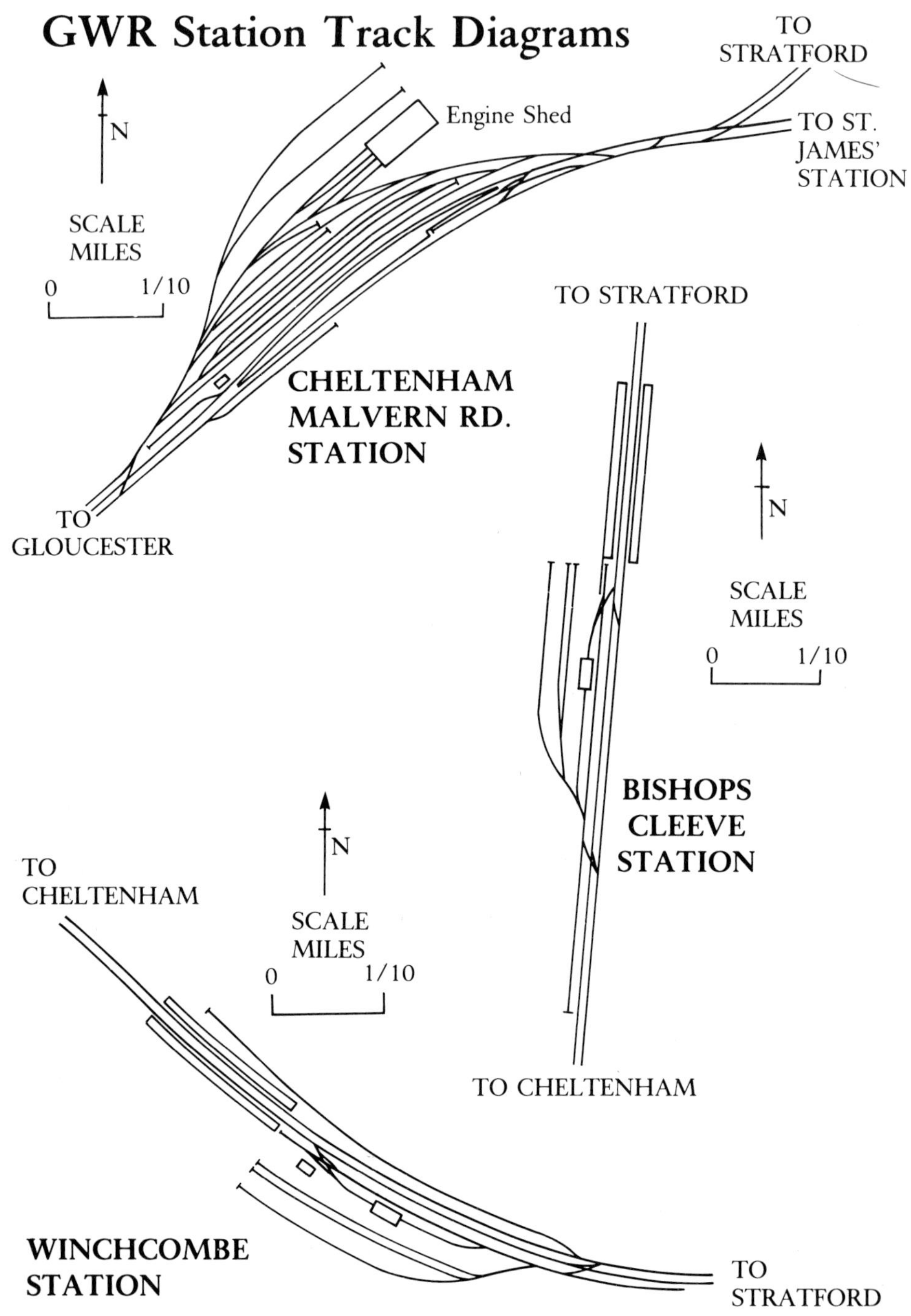

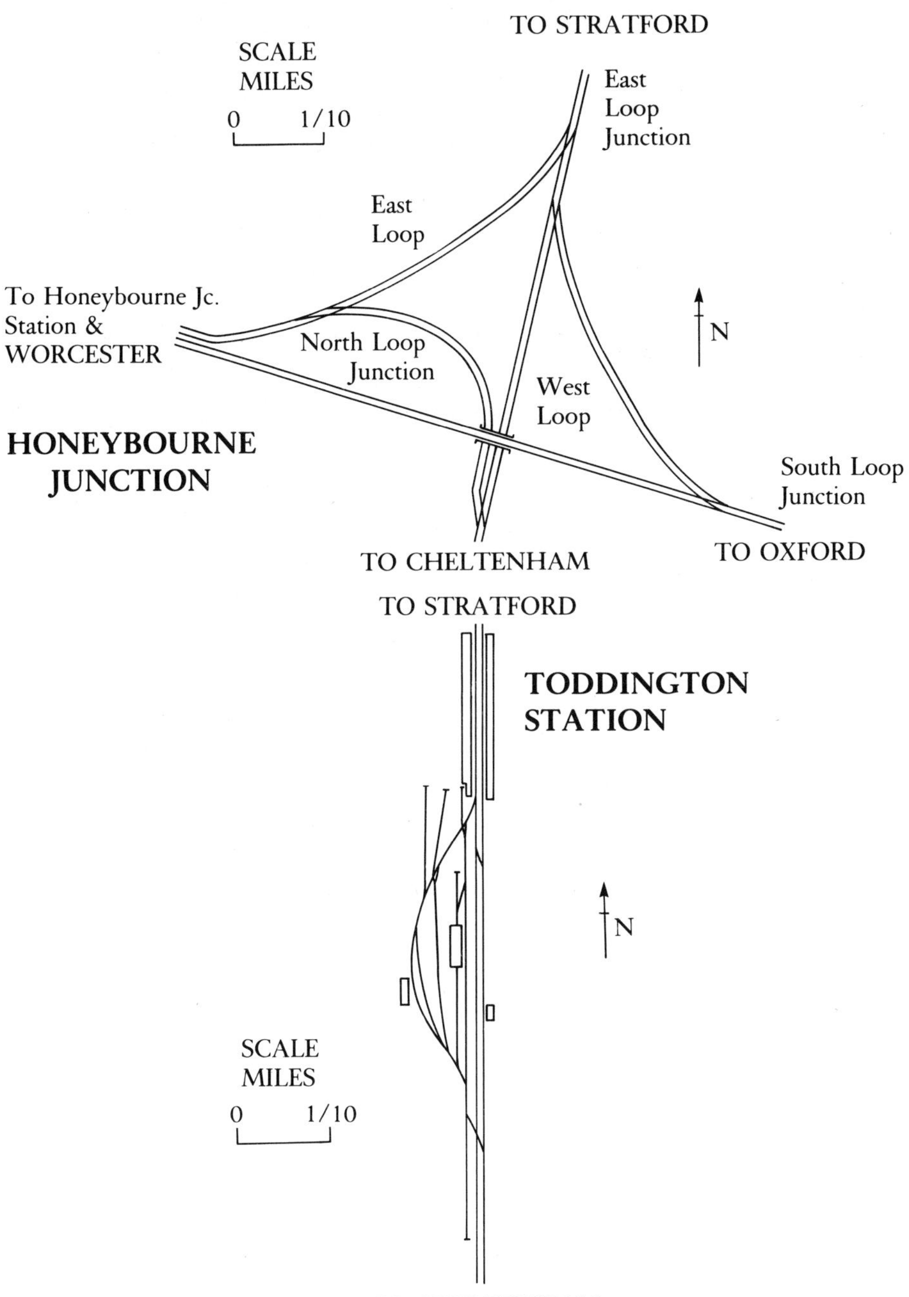

TO STRATFORD
SCALE
MILES
0   1/10
East
Loop
Junction
East
Loop
To Honeybourne Jc.
Station &
WORCESTER
North Loop
Junction
West
Loop
N
HONEYBOURNE
JUNCTION
South Loop
Junction
TO CHELTENHAM
TO OXFORD
TO STRATFORD
TODDINGTON
STATION
N
SCALE
MILES
0   1/10
TO CHELTENHAM

GREAT WESTERN RAILWAY.

Circular No. $\frac{F.\ 1654.}{R.\ 1283.}$

PADDINGTON STATION,
28th MAY, 1906.

Cheltenham and Honeybourne Line.

With reference to Circular No. $\frac{F.\ 1556}{R.\ 1263}$ dated January 25th, 1905, the Cheltenham and Honeybourne New Line is now completed as far as Bishop's Cleeve, and on **Friday, June 1st, 1906, Cretton Halt (to pick up and set down Passengers only), Gotherington and Bishop's Cleeve Stations** will be opened for traffic. It is expected that the remaining portion of the New Line will be opened through to Cheltenham on August 1st.

PASSENGER AND PARCELS TRAFFIC.

The Service for Passenger and Parcels Traffic on the New Line will be worked by Rail Motor Service (one class only), and 1st, 2nd and 3rd class Fares between Gotherington and Bishop's Cleeve Stations on the New Line, and Stations beyond Honeybourne, will be put into operation, enabling Passengers to travel by Rail Motor on the New Line and 1st, 2nd or 3rd class by Ordinary Train to and from Honeybourne.

Through Fares and Rates will be supplied as required.

Parcels may be booked through to and from your Station and Gotherington and Bishop's Cleeve Stations at the Clearing House scale.

Insert in alphabetical order Gotherington and Bishop's Cleeve Stations on your Local Stations Card.

GOODS TRAFFIC.

Extensive lists of Rates are being issued with Gotherington and Bishop's Cleeve, but if any beyond those provided are required, application must be made to your District Goods Manager.

The Company will not for the present undertake cartage at these places, and Rates must not be quoted as including this service.

Contractor's Locomotives Used on the Construction of the Honeybourne Line

Manning Wardle locomotives used by Walter Scott & Middleton Ltd. on construction work 1902—1906:

Builders No.	Date built	Class	Name
583	1876	M	*Ciceter*
892	1883	D	*Luli*
899	1884	M	*Bradford*
971	1885	K	*Corea*
1047	1888	M	*Disley*
1059	1888	K	*Bertha*
1425	1898	L	*Stublic*
1447	1899	L	*Sirdar*
1502	1900	Spl. K	*Buller*
1525	1902	M	*Pallion*

All locomotives were 0-6-0 saddle tank engines, except No. 892 which was an 0-4-0 saddle tank. One other locomotive was used, possibly No. 678 of 1877, class K, "*Rugby*".

Honeybourne Line reconstruction. GWR 6 ton hand operated crane stands at the Railway Company's boundary, May 1982, pointing towards Winchcombe, which should be reached with permanent way in 1985 ready for public services the following year. (P.D. Nicholson)

A Cross-country diesel multiple unit set passes through Toddington station with the 12.25 hrs Birmingham (Snow Hill) to Carmarthen on 27th February 1960. Now the centre of operations for the Gloucestershire Warwickshire Railway, this station is sure to become the scene of greater activity than any other period in its history. (D.H. Ballantyne)

One scene that can never be repeated — 'Aberdare' class 2-6-0 heads a goods working at Cheltenham Spa (Malvern Road) station in March 1945, travelling northwards. In the background, alongside Malvern shed is another member of the same class, No. 2638. This locomotive had a broken crankpin and never returned to service, departing for Swindon in September, destined for scrapping. (W. Potter)

Bibliography

Titled Trains of the Western; C.J. Allen. Ian Allan
Board of Trade Inspectors' Reports
Bradshaw's Railway Guides
British Rail Main Line Gradient Profiles; Ian Allan
Regional History of the Railways of Great Britain: Vol.13 Thames & Severn: R. Christiansen. David & Charles
An Historical Survey of Selected Great Western Stations: Vol.3; R.H. Clark. Oxford Publishing Company
Closed Stations & Goods Depots; C.R. Clinker. Avon-Anglia
Track Layout Diagrams, Sections 28, 30 and 35; R.A. Cooke
Stratford & Midland Junction Railway; J.M. Dunn. Oakwood Press
Industrial Locomotives of Central Southern England; R.K. Hateley. Industrial Railway Society
The Oxford, Worcester & Wolverhampton Railway; S.C. Jenkins & H.I. Quayle. Oakwood Press
An Historical Survey of Great Western Engine Sheds 1837—1947; E. Lyons & E. Mountford. Oxford Publishing Company
An Historical Survey of Great Western Engine Sheds 1947; E. Lyons Oxford Publishing Company
History of the Great Western Railway; E.T. MacDermot/C.R. Clinker, O.S. Nock. Ian Allan
Bristol & Gloucester Railway; C.G. Maggs. Oakwood Press
Midland & South Western Junction Railway; C.G. Maggs. David & Charles
Manning Wardle & Co. Ltd; F.W. Mabbott. Thomas Aleksandr
Railways of the Cotswolds; C.G. Maggs. Peter Nicholson
Britain's Railways at War 1939-1945; O.S. Nock. Ian Allan
GWR Steam; O.S. Nock. David & Charles
Locomotives of the Great Western Railway; R.C.T.S.
A Pictorial Record of Great Western Railway Architecture; A. Vaughan Oxford Publishing Company
Magazines and Newspapers: The Engineer; Engineering; Great Western Railway Magazine; Railway Magazine; Railway Observer; Railway Times; SLS Journal; GWRS Newsletter; The Cornishman; Cheltenham Chronicle & Graphic; Cheltenham Examiner; Cheltenham Free Press; Gloucestershire Echo.

Acknowledgements
Grateful acknowledgements for assistance are due to: D.J. Andrews; D.H. Ballantyne; T. Bazeley; D. Heathcote; H.G.W. Household; S. James; L.B. Lapper; W. Potter; J.R. Robson; D.R. Steggles; R.J. Washington; G. Wigg and J.R. Wood of Cheltenham Library.

....AND THE STORY GOES ON

Unquenchable enthusiasm and a desire to put things back as they should be is the driving force behind the Gloucestershire Warwickshire Railway project.

Formed in the mid 1970s, a pressure group to keep the line open developed into a preservation project, which took occupation at a bleak and derelict Toddington Yard during 1981. The GWR now has the freehold on fifteen miles of track bed stretching from Broadway to Cheltenham with the possibility of extending further north in the future. Buildings have since been restored, track has been bought and laid and steam trains shuttle back and forth giving pleasure to thousands. The achievements of the GWR are too many to mention here but if you want to find out more or would like to take an active part in this exciting project write to:— The Secretary, Toddington Station, Toddington, Glos.